RELIGIONS
OF
JAPAN

Religious Traditions of the World

Titles available from Waveland Press

RELIGIONS OF JAPAN

*Many Traditions Within
One Sacred Way*

H. BYRON EARHART

WAVELAND
PRESS, INC.

Prospect Heights, Illinois

For information about this book, write or call:
    Waveland Press, Inc.
    P.O. Box 400
    Prospect Heights, Illinois 60070
    (847) 634-0081

*All photos are by the author with the exception of that on page 78,
which is reproduced here courtesy of Dr. Robert J. Smith.*

for Mircea Eliade

and

Joseph M. Kitagawa

Contents

Preface

For more than twenty years I have enjoyed my professional field of specialization, studying Japanese religion. Some of this time has been spent in Japan doing research on specific aspects of Japanese religion; much of the rest of the time has been spent teaching and writing on this subject. The present book is an attempt to share with others my fascination for its amazing variety. This rich treasury of religion in Japan makes it difficult to limit this work to those aspects that can be treated in a few chapters. But this book is intended as a brief introduction to Japanese religion, not a comprehensive interpretation. I have therefore tried to explore whatever is of greatest help and interest to the person first reading about Japanese religion. To the extent that these chapters help the reader appreciate the richness of the Japanese tradition, my purpose is fulfilled.

Included in this book are several features to assist the reader in becoming acquainted with Japan and Japanese religion. A map shows the location of the Japanese islands in relationship to Asia and identifies major cities and some religious centers mentioned in the text (page 8). A table of Japanese religious history provides chronology in Japanese periods and Western dates, with major cultural and religious features (pages 5–7). (This table provides a convenient overview of Japanese religious history that can be used in at least three ways: first, before reading the book, to get a bird's eye view of the subject; second, while reading the book, to place particular materials in historical context; and third, after reading the book, to review and unify all the materials.) At the end of the book a glossary lists key terms in the study of Japanese religion, with brief definitions or identifications; each glossary term is printed in boldface where it first appears in the text. A selected reading list enables the interested reader to pursue this subject in other publications.

H. B. E.

■

Acknowledgments

T his book is dedicated to Mircea Eliade and Joseph M. Kitagawa, who were my dissertation advisors at the University of Chicago; their teaching and help, both during graduate school and subsequently, have been invaluable for all my work, including this book.

Many people deserve special thanks for having helped bring this present work to completion. My son David carefully read the first draft, making valuable suggestions for improving it.

Preparing the manuscript and making changes was simplified by the use of a computer, which was made possible by a number of persons and agencies at Western Michigan University. The manuscript was first entered on the word processor of the History Department, thanks to Dr. Ernst Breisach, chair of the History Department, and Mrs. Opal Ellis, secretary. Mark S. Liberacki, Systems Specialist for the College of Arts and Sciences, was responsible for transmitting this input to the main academic computer. The Computer Center and its staff of consultants provided the facilities and assistance that enabled me to use the computer to edit the manuscript. Dr. Thomas VanValey of the Sociology Department was my efficient tutor in text editing.

Western Michigan University, through its Faculty Research Fund, has from time to time supported my research in Japanese religion; although no direct support was provided for this book, acknowledgment is gratefully noted for helping make possible the previous research on which this book is based.

The editorial and production staff transformed the manuscript into this published book. Special thanks go to John Loudon, Kathy Reigstad, and Thomas Dorsaneo.

H. B. E.

■

Table of Japanese Religious History

Chronology of Japanese Historical Periods and Western Dates	Major Cultural and Religious Features

RELIGIOUS CUSTOMS IN EARLY JAPAN

Prehistoric
(to sixth century A.D.)

Transition from hunting-gathering culture to rice agriculture and small villages and development of Japanese religious practices—ancient Shinto and kami, seasonal festivals and agricultural fertility—spirits of the dead; and divine descent of imperial family.

CHINESE AND INDIAN INFLUENCE ON JAPANESE RELIGION

Taika (645–710)

Nara (710–784)

Chinese culture influential in development of written language, centralized government, first permanent capital at Nara; introduction of Confucianism, religious Taoism, and Buddhism; Shinto becomes more formally organized, and all traditions interact.

THE FLOWERING OF JAPANESE BUDDHISM

Heian (794–1185)

Kamakura (1185–1333)

Capital moves from Nara to Kyoto, and elegant life develops among court and nobility; Shingon and Tendai sects of Buddhism founded during Heian period; rise to power of military dictator and warriors from new center of power at Kamakura; during Kamakura period Pure Land, Nichiren, and Zen sects of Buddhism founded; Shinto becomes more highly organized and develops eclectic teachings.

RELIGION IN MEDIEVAL JAPAN

Muromachi (1333–1568)

Momoyama (1568–1600)

Tokugawa (1600–1867)

Much civil war and strife until Tokugawa government gains control, unifying and stabilizing the country; development of cities and merchant class; Buddhist denominations develop from earlier sects, and Shinto refines systems of eclectic teachings; Christianity (Roman Catholicism) is introduced and enjoys brief success before being banned; Confucian teachings provide the social rationale for the Tokugawa ruling system, and families are required to belong to Buddhist temples.

JAPAN ENTERS THE MODERN WORLD

Meiji (1868–1911)

Taisho (1912–1925)

Showa (1926—   )

Transition from feudal rule to modern nation-state, end of rule by military dictators with new parliamentary government at Tokyo; rapid development of education and industry; in Meiji times required membership in Buddhist temples dropped, ban on Christianity lifted (and Protestant and Catholic Christianity introduced), Shinto made a state religion and New Religions become significant movements; after 1945 and Japan's defeat in World War II, development of more democratic policies, including a new constitution and complete religious freedom; Shinto's role as a state religion is removed, with all religions enjoying complete freedom; Japan rebuilds and becomes a major economic and political power; Shinto and Buddhism slowly recover strength after World War II, New Religions become the most rapidly developing religious force, and there is widespread secularism and religious indifference.

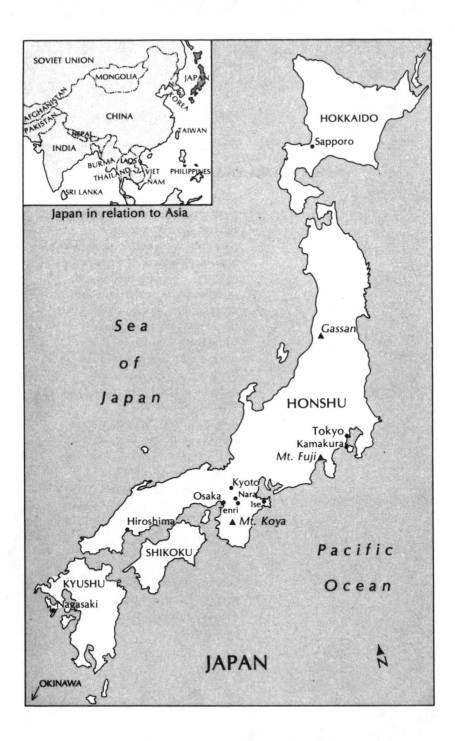

Japan in relation to Asia

SOVIET UNION

MONGOLIA

JAPAN

AFGHANISTAN
PAKISTAN

CHINA

KOREA

TAIWAN

INDIA

NEPAL

BURMA LAOS

THAILAND VIET
NAM

PHILIPPINES

SRI LANKA

HOKKAIDO

Sapporo

Sea

of

Japan

Gassan

HONSHU

Tokyo
Kamakura
Mt. Fuji

Kyoto
Osaka
Nara
Tenri
Ise

Hiroshima

Mt. Koya

SHIKOKU

Pacific

Ocean

KYUSHU

Nagasaki

JAPAN

N

OKINAWA

■

CHAPTER I

Introduction: Japan and Japanese Religion

People outside of Japan know more about recent Japan and its technological achievements—automobiles, cameras, and electronics—than about its traditional culture and religion. But as proud as the Japanese are of their technological and commercial success, they have not become completely "Westernized," for Japanese culture dates back several thousand years, and Japanese people are equally proud of the distinctive culture they inherit from the past—its language, national identity, arts, and religious traditions. This book will focus on the distinctively Japanese religious heritage (which will be called Japanese religion), introducing the individual religious traditions and interpreting the general world view created by all these traditions together.

In order to treat Japan's religious heritage, it is necessary to deal with some aspects of Japan other than religion. In this first chapter we will look primarily at the two elements of the term *religions of Japan*—what defines Japan as a national and cultural unit and what religious traditions are found in Japan. The second chapter will describe how Japanese religion developed historically from the earliest times to the present. The third and fourth chapters will interpret how Japanese religion is organized into a total way of life, providing not only objects of worship but a complete understanding of the human career. The fifth chapter shows how Japanese religion has functioned concretely, giving two examples of the dynamics of Japanese religion in action. The final chapter looks more closely at religion in contemporary Japan.

What Is Japan?

Japan has many aspects, some concrete and visible, some more abstract and intangible. Japan is the land that is the living space of the country; it is the people who live in the land and constitute its citizenry; it is the economic activity sustaining the life of the people individually and collectively; it is the nation as a political entity, both as the government forming the state and as the loyalty of the people supporting the state; it is the Japanese language, spoken by no other people in the world; it is the many art forms and the aesthetic sensibilities that characterize Japanese culture; and it is the pattern of individual religions, and beliefs and practices that make up the Japanese religious tradition. All of these aspects are closely related parts of the total experience of Japan. For convenience we will view each of them separately, looking first at the components of "Japan" and then turning to the religious dimension of the Japanese experience.

When we look at a map, the first thing we notice about Japan is that it is a curved semicircle of islands off the coast of the Asian continent. This geographical situation of Japan in relation to Asia has played a great role in the formation of a distinctive Japanese culture and a separate national experience, because Japan was close enough to receive periodic influences yet far enough away to mold those influences into a peculiarly Japanese way of life. Some traditional accounts view the beginning of the Japanese nation as the creation of the Japanese islands six thousand years ago by the **kami*** (deities), but most modern historians consider "Japan" to date from a little more than two thousand years ago.

From about that time, there began to emerge a distinctive group of people (the Japanese people), a particular way of life (Japanese culture), and a specific national identity (the Japanese nation). Throughout the centuries, many "borrowed" elements have entered Japan from the outside, and many changes have taken place within Japanese society, but underneath all these changes has been a strong sense of the continuity of Japan as an ongoing tradition.

---

*Terms defined in the Glossary are printed in boldface where they first appear in the text.

The most concrete aspect of Japan is the Japanese islands: at present, Japanese territory includes four major islands (from south to north, Kyushu, Shikoku, Honshu, and Hokkaido) and numerous smaller islands (such as Okinawa). In earliest times, there were no clear-cut boundaries, but the people and culture that came to be known as Japanese formed first in the areas close to Korea, on the islands of Kyushu and southwest Honshu. Gradually the people of southwestern Japan came to control all the Japanese islands, and their life-style formed the basis for the culture found in these islands today.

Although today the Japanese people are viewed as a single nationality, they share a common ancestry with other Asian peoples. Early Japan was probably inhabited by people who entered from the northern Asian continent and from the areas south of Japan. The Japanese people, however, see themselves as much more than merely Asians who inhabit a particular place. From ancient times the Japanese have perceived themselves in terms of the mythology of their descent from the first people who inhabited the Japanese islands, thought to be created by the kami. Although this mythology is not always taken so literally today, there remains in the people of Japan a strong sense of self-identity as distinct from all other people.

To "be Japanese" means much more than to be born of Japanese parents and to learn Japanese customs. It means also to be part of a family system. By contrast with the sense of individualism in Western countries like the United States, Japanese people tend to view themselves and to behave as members of a family more than as individuals. Generally speaking, in Japanese society there is a greater sense of belonging to social groups than there is in Western countries, whether family, university, or company. And this sense of belonging is not just an abstract notion but is channeled through specific relationships: children's loyalty to parents, a student's respect for a professor (even long after graduation), and the cooperation with fellow workers in a particular division of a larger company.

Some scholars think that the present emphasis in Japan on large extended families and on social cooperation (rather than individualism) is closely linked to the pattern of rice agriculture in Japan. The economic life of the earliest inhabitants of the Japanese islands was a combination of hunting and gathering, especially collecting shellfish along the ocean shore. More than two thousand years ago, this hunt-ing-gathering pattern gradually gave way to agriculture; in Japan rice became the staff of life, as it did in many other Asian countries. Rice has been an extremely important feature of the Japanese econo-my, closely related to social life and an important symbol of the blessings of nature. Rice requires large amounts of hand labor but also gives rather large yields. It was especially rice that allowed the Japanese people to develop more permanent large-scale settlements, and on the basis of this rice agriculture, a form of feudal govern-ment emerged, with nobility and wealthy landowners at the top of the society and relatively poor farmers and tenants at the bottom. The poorest farmers did not always have rice to eat (eating instead foods not so valuable as a cash crop), but they had to pay taxes in rice, which was almost the same as money. Many of the seasonal rituals in Japan are marked by the various seasons and events con-nected with the growing and harvesting of rice.

Japan is well known for its rapid technological and commercial development after World War II, but the foundations for this suc-cess go back at least several hundred years, when widespread trade arose between urban centers and rural regions. Not only foods such as rice, rice wine (*sake*), and soy sauce, but also textiles and fertilizer, were important in this large trade network and its large-scale bank-ing system. From the late nineteenth century, Japan deliberately set out on a course of promoting education, technology, and industry in order to compete with the West. Since World War II Japanese busi-ness has combined imported technical information and manage-ment techniques with native ingenuity and innovation to create one of the most competitive industrial-commercial forces in the world, emphasizing high quality at low prices. A few decades ago Japan still suffered the bad reputation of being a "borrower" of every-thing, from culture to technology, but nowadays Western countries ask how they can borrow technical breakthroughs and management practices from Japan.

The system of government has gone through many significant changes in Japanese history. In the earliest times, the clan, or large family was an important social and political unit, and the most re-vered family line was that of the imperial family, thought to be de-scended from the divine creators of the Japanese islands. Some of the earliest records of Japan are Chinese writings that describe rule by empresses; however, rule by empresses soon gave way to a hereditary line of emperors. These emperors were the symbolic heads of state and national ceremonies but did not rule directly. Cabinets and ministries administered governments; as Chinese influence dominated Japan after about the sixth century, Chinese models of centralized government were adopted, but gradually the Chinese models were replaced by Japanese adaptations.

Until the twelfth century, a lively imperial court and a wealthy nobility ruled the country and presided over an aristocratic life-style that is still remembered with nostalgia today. Power gradually shifted to the military. In the twelfth century the military gained control of the country and, for all practical purposes, became the rulers, replacing the symbolic figure of the emperor and also the nobility. Much blood was shed in the quest for military supremacy among competing feudal powers, and finally in the seventeenth century, the country was unified by a military ruler (**shogun**) who received allegiance and tribute from regional feudal lords. Gradually the feudal way of life was weakened by internal changes in the Japanese economy and society and by external pressures of foreign governments that sought to open Japan to trade. These forces combined to help bring an end to the feudal style of government in 1867, when the modern nation-state of Japan was formed: feudal domains and social class divisions were abolished and there came to be truly national control over regional prefectures (divisions similar to states in the United States). Some democratic ideas were developed during the early twentieth century, but major democratic changes in Japanese society were brought about after 1945 following Japan's defeat in World War II. Today, the emperor is still respected as a symbol of the nation, but Japan is a democratic country with a parliamentary government headed by a prime minister.

One of the most distinctive features of the Japanese heritage is the Japanese language. The earliest origins of Japanese are lost in history, much as are the origins of the Japanese people. Whatever the ancient influences upon the Japanese language, it is not spoken by any other people. Unlike the closely related Romance languages such as Italian, French, and Spanish, the Japanese language is not closely related to languages of neighboring countries. For example, Japanese is quite different from Chinese: spoken Japanese does not feature a distinct pattern of tones, as does spoken Chinese. One of the most interesting characteristics of Japanese—and one quite difficult for Westerners to learn—is the many levels of politeness expressed. The Japanese language is "hierarchical," in the sense that different verbs, verb endings, nouns, and other forms must be used depending on the hierarchical social relation between speaker and listener. A professor will use quite different language to speak to a student than the student will use to speak to the professor.

Japanese was not a written language until Chinese writing symbols ("characters" or "ideographs") were borrowed. These Chinese symbols or characters are identical (or slightly abbreviated) in Japan (and in Korea). But in Japan, two phonetic systems were used to retain the structure and grammar of spoken Japanese while borrowing elements of written Chinese. Although some key elements are shared with languages using Chinese characters, a person must learn the phonetic system and grammar of Japanese in order to understand the relations between these elements and written Japanese. This language may be seen as an isolated pocket by outsiders, but to the Japanese people it is a proud expression of their national heritage. The Japanese have translated extensively, so that today they can read in their own language a wide variety of materials—from the Western classics to recent writing in science and social science.

Japanese art has absorbed considerable outside influence but still expresses an aesthetic sensitivity that is peculiar to Japan. The seventh-century poetry anthology *Manyoshu* displays some of the same themes—love of nature and appreciation of subtle human emotions—that are found in poetry and literature even today. Nature is a major subject in poetry and also in graphic art. Nature is not depicted, as it often is in the West, as the creation of God—rather, nature itself is practically divine. Landscape painting is one of the favorite forms of graphic art: mountains, rivers, trees, waterfalls and other natural scenes grace paintings, folding screens, fans, and woodblock prints. Even popular decorative art from the sixteenth century selected natural phenomena, such as beetles or the cicada, for small carvings.

Not only does art praise nature, but it also focuses attention on the shifting seasons and subtle emotional responses to nature. In fact, the role of poetry in Japan contrasts sharply with the Western pattern in which God inspires poetry and art; in Japan it is poetry that moves the deities. The tenth-century *Kokinshu* (*Collection of An-*

cient and Modern Poetry) states that Japanese poetry "moves heaven and earth, and stirs to pity the invisible demons and gods."[1]* The twelfth-century *Tale of Genji*—sometimes considered the world's first novel—is an artistic chronicling of the life and loves of the nobility and the imperial court; equally important as the message of a love poem is the paper on which it is written and the fragrance of the perfume on the paper. These aesthetic nuances live on today, for the *Manyoshu* and the *Tale of Genji* are not historical curiosities but are loved for their intrinsic artistic imagery and are still models for contemporary works.

It is difficult to capture the "essence" of Japanese art, which, like all cultural forms, has changed considerably through time. But one theme that has endured from prehistoric ages down to the present is an emphasis on the natural qualities of artistic materials. More often than not, the texture of clay, the grain of wood, the fibers of paper, are not covered up but are valued as an integral part of the artistic creation. This is seen in prehistoric and ancient pottery; it is also reflected in great architectural achievements such as the **Shinto shrine** buildings of Ise, where natural (unpainted) wood and thatch roof complement each other in stark simplicity against the background of a pebble-filled courtyard and majestic evergreen woods. Others may prefer the abstract quality of **Zen** gardens with raked sand and stones, where a person may meditate on these monuments of permanence contrasting with the impermanence of human life. These examples have been taken mainly from aristocratic and elite culture, but even folk toys are often made out of natural materials. One of the great contrasts in Japanese art is between the more refined and subdued traditions already mentioned and the more gaudy and bright colors associated with some shrines and temples and much of popular culture. There is no room here to indicate the variety of art forms and their different moods—from the various forms of theater and puppetry to the art of the tea ceremony and other distinctive Japanese creations.

Japan has a whole treasure house of its own art forms, of which the Japanese people are quite proud. But we should recognize that modern Japanese artists are cosmopolitan, from woodblock print artists to painters and architects. Modern Japanese novels have been

*Notes are listed together at the end of the text, beginning on p. 135.

praised throughout the world, and not long ago Yasunari Kawabata became the first Japanese novelist to win a Nobel Prize in literature.

What Is Japanese Religion?

Now that we have looked briefly at Japan itself—its land, people, economic activity, government, language, and arts—let us turn to the religions of Japan. *Japanese religion* is the general term we will use to refer collectively to all of the following religious phenomena: the half dozen religious traditions found in Japan and their component parts; various beliefs and practices observed by the Japanese people; and the overall world view that is shared by these organized religions and in which these beliefs and practices are grounded. We will look at these various phenomena one by one, starting with the more easily recognizable traditions. Many religious traditions are found in Japan: the formal religions of Shinto, **Buddhism, Christianity**, and numerous **New Religions**; the less formal traditions of **Confucianism** and **Taoism**; and the practices and beliefs of **folk religion**.

Shinto is the most ancient of all Japanese religious traditions, having grown out of prehistoric Japanese beliefs and practices—especially those revering nature. Shinto means, literally, "the way of many kami" (spirits or deities), and usually these kami either helped create aspects of nature or are themselves expressed in natural forms. Families, and villages as groups of families, worshiped local kami as the source of blessing for agriculture (especially rice) and their group life. The power of the kami, as the force behind and within life, was seen to reside within natural objects.

One of the chief characteristics of Shinto is the close and intimate relationship between humans and kami. (Kami can refer to one or many "deities"). In fact, kami may even merge with human beings, such as, for example, the "divine" emperor and the "holy" founders of religious movements. Kami are also quite comfortable in the home: the traditional house still contains a Shinto-style altar for kami, and offerings of food are presented at this altar by the family members. Kami are everywhere, filling the landscape and inhabiting the home.

Generally the Japanese people have seen kami to be the source of life and blessing and have approached kami to pray for blessings and give thanks. In Shinto great emphasis is placed on cleanliness and purification; Shinto shrines provide water for people to purify their hands and mouths before coming into contact with kami. Most Shinto rituals begin with an invocation of the presence of kami and with a "sending off" of kami. Most of the occasions for such rituals are seasonal festivals, often linked to the agricultural work cycle. This direct appreciation of nature and sincere acceptance of the blessing of kami is favored, rather than the development of complicated doctrine and abstract philosophy. Leading a pure and sincere life under the blessing of many kami is at the heart of Shinto ideals.

Shinto arose gradually within Japanese culture, but Buddhism was founded in distant India by the **Buddha** and had to cross both China and Korea to arrive in Japan. The Buddha founded a way of life aimed at eliminating suffering through the realization of **enlightenment**—an awakening to a higher peace beyond human suffering. By the time of Buddhism's entry into Japan in the sixth century A.D., about a thousand years had passed since its founding. During that millennium, Buddhism had developed an elaborate monastic community, had come to serve as the religious rationale for the state, and had practiced rituals for the funerals and memorials of the dead.

In Japan Buddhism exists on a number of levels for various groups of people. For example, the philosophical tradition of Indian Buddhism is preserved mainly by and for scholars, whereas the monastic tradition has gradually given way to a hereditary system of married priests. However, for most people today, the primary significance of Buddhism lies in the rituals for memorializing spirits of the family **ancestors** and the secondary significance in seasonal and special visits to **temples** for various blessings.

In Japan, Buddhism presents an interesting variety of institutional and popular forms. The goal of Indian Buddhism, enlightenment (**nirvana**), is well known in Japan through the Zen sect's quest for awakening (*satori*): Zen emphasizes meditation in order to still the mind and bring both mind and body to a state of serenity and peace. A number of other sects were transmitted from China to Japan or developed in Japan. Generally, people are less concerned with enlightenment than with the safe passage of themselves (and their ancestors) to Buddhist paradise. Two practices are especially important in assuring passage to paradise: reciting praise to **Amida** (one of the chief Buddhist saints) by a person during one's lifetime; and, after one's death, the family's performance or supervision of funeral and memorial rites for the spirit of the deceased.

On the popular level, the most important role of Buddhism is in memorializing the spirits of the ancestors in the home. In recent times almost every main family (headed by a first son) has had a Buddhist altar, a kind of cabinet in which are enshrined the wooden memorial tablets representing the transformed spirits of the family dead. On the anniversary of a family member's death, the family made offerings to the ancestors and might have called in a Buddhist priest to recite scriptures. The lofty notion of enlightenment and other complex doctrines dominated the monasteries, while more popular notions of entering paradise and venerating ancestors flourished in the home.

Taoism and Confucianism both developed in China and are less formal traditions than Shinto and Buddhism. Taoism and Confucianism are the two major philosophical and religious traditions arising in China, but we will be concerned mainly with their role within Japanese culture. Taoism means literally the "way" (*tao* in Chinese), in the sense of the way of the universe or nature. The Taoist tradition is best known in the form of a Chinese philosophical and semimystical writing, the *Tao Te Ching*. Contrasted with philosophical Taoism are the many practices related to the calendar (indicating days of good and bad luck), divination, and other folk beliefs that came to be known as religious Taoism.

In Japan it was mainly this loose collection of beliefs and practices called religious Taoism that had greatest influence. Although Taoism never existed as a separate religious tradition in Japan, by the eighth century a bureau of divination was patterned on a similar bureau at the Chinese court. Gradually these Chinese notions of interpreting the workings of nature and harmonizing human life with nature came to be linked to Japanese notions about the kami, nature, and rituals. For example, most Japanese rituals are performed in accordance with the Chinese calendar, which incorporates many of the features of religious Taoism. The Japanese bureau of divination quickly passed out of existence, but many of the notions of religious Taoism about lucky and unlucky days and means of divining fortunes became part of popular culture and are still practiced today (though many Japanese people do not know their Taoist origins). In this sense, Taoism is more an indirect influence on Japanese culture than a formal religious tradition. Probably no Japanese person would call him- or herself a Taoist, even though Taoist notions may have unconsciously been used in selecting a proper day for a wedding or a funeral.

Confucianism has a much more definite origin and development than does Taoism. Taoism grew out of various writings and popular beliefs and practices, but Confucianism was based on the ideas of the historical man **Confucius** (551–479 B.C.). Confucius was a Chinese teacher who set forth his ideas about the nature of human virtue and the kind of human relationships that should be found in a harmonious society. Although he was not successful in persuading rulers of the many smaller kingdoms of his time to follow his teachings, once China was unified in the Han dynasty (202 B.C.–A.D. 220), the ideas of Confucius were elaborated and systematized into a rationale for society and government. Confucianism is the name given the philosophy of life and ethical system first taught by Confucius and later systematized by followers and the government. He emphasized a return to virtue and an overall social harmony based on proper relationships among people in terms of their social roles. Two of the most important of these hierarchical relationships are father-son and ruler-citizen: the father and ruler should be benevolent; the son and citizen should be obedient. In Japan, Confucianism as a philosophy of life served to legitimize society as a whole (reinforcing loyalty to a hereditary imperial line) and basic social units (especially the family). In some periods, forms of Confucian teachings tended to dominate all Japanese society (particularly in the Tokugawa period, 1600–1867). Confucian ideas continue even today to influence Japanese notions of family and society.

Christianity, the dominant religion of Europe, spread to other lands, such as India and China, even within the first few centuries after it was founded. But Christianity did not reach Japanese shores until the Spanish Jesuit missionary Saint Francis Xavier arrived in 1549. For about the next hundred years, Catholic misionaries overcame tremendous obstacles—language difficulties and political turmoil—to convert a significant number of the Japanese to Christianity. During the seventeenth century the government banned

Christianity and subjected Christians to one of the most cruel persecutions the church has ever suffered. It was thought that Christianity had been completely stamped out, but some Christians continued to practice some Christian rituals in their homes in secret. In the middle of the nineteenth century, when Japan again opened its doors to outside trade and culture, Catholicism once more entered Japan, as did Protestantism for the first time.

Christianity has played a relatively minor role in Japanese religion, partly because it entered Japan so much later than other traditions, and partly because Christianity has tended to remain a "foreign" tradition rather than blending freely with other Japanese traditions. In many crucial features Christianity differs from Japanese religion: Christianity emphasizes worship of one true God, whereas Japanese religion accepts many deities (both kami and Buddhas); Christianity preaches forgiveness of sins, whereas Japanese religion practices purification of impurity; Christianity demands total commitment to one religion, whereas Japanese religion accepts simultaneous participation in a number of religious traditions. The sharp difference between Christianity and the Japanese religious heritage helps explain why less than one percent of the Japanese population today are members of Christian churches. But although membership is low, Christianity has had considerable influence in Japan through widespread reading of the Bible and through pioneering social reform programs.

Folk religion is less easily identified than these other traditions, which are either formal religions (with priests, buildings, and rituals) or at least written traditions (with texts, commentaries, and scholars). In fact, folk religion can best be characterized as the religious beliefs and practices that occur outside institutional religion, apart from written traditions. Folk religion often incorporates parts of the more formal traditions in its practices but continues them apart from an institutional religion or written tradition. Many of the beliefs and practices of folk religion are part of the oral tradition handed down in families and carried on by villages in seasonal observances and village festivals. For example, in traditional Japan many rituals connected with the growing of rice were performed by families and villages as part of their local culture. Sometimes Buddhist priests and Shinto priests participated in these ceremonies; at other times the villagers were able to carry out the festivals themselves. The celebration of the New Year in the home is a good example of folk religion. A family observed many folk practices without any assistance from institutional religion: placed pine boughs at their gate, set up special decorations within the home, and even cooked special New Year's foods. Much of the dynamics of Japanese religion takes place in terms of such folk religion.

In addition to the traditions that appeared in Japan from prehistoric times to several centuries ago, many New Religions arose during the past century and a half. These New Religions are "new" in the sense of being new arrangements of elements from most of the other traditions. Usually a New Religion was founded by a charismatic individual who had a revelatory experience or rediscovered the power of earlier teachings and practices and arranged (or rearranged) such experiences, teachings, and practices into a separate religious group after a sufficient number of people had been attracted to the founder and the founder's message. These New Religions have been very active in seeking members and have been successful also through use of publishing and other mass media.

The earliest New Religion to gain a widespread following, **Tenrikyo** (literally, "the religion of divine wisdom"), was founded in 1838 by a woman, Mrs. Miki Nakayama. She was possessed by a creator deity while she participated in a healing ceremony for her son, and this experience led to a lifelong commitment to teach the message of this divinity; she taught people to remove the impurities or "dust" from their souls and return to this deity in order to lead a joyous life. Tenrikyo developed a nationwide system of religious branches, and its headquarters at the city of Tenri (near Nara) is a famous pilgrimage site for Tenrikyo members.

Probably the most powerful New Religion today is **Soka Gakkai**, which was founded shortly before World War II. It was refounded about 1950 and attracted millions of followers in the space of about ten years. Soka Gakkai focuses on the power in the **Lotus Sutra**, a traditional Buddhist scripture of the **Nichiren** tradition. According to Soka Gakkai, members who commit themselves exclusively to practices of this tradition are able to solve all problems by placing their faith in the Lotus Sutra and chanting the title of the Lotus Sutra.

Tenrikyo and Soka Gakkai are two examples of the larger New Religions, of which there are several dozen. Including the smaller

New Religions, there are several hundred such movements in modern Japan, making them one of the most conspicuous forces on the contemporary religious scene.

Many Traditions Within One Sacred Way

We have now looked at seven major areas of Japanese religion—the individual traditions of Shinto, Buddhism, Taoism, Confucianism, Christianity, folk religion, and New Religions. However, Japanese religion cannot be understood simply by separating it into individual components, because Japanese people do not "belong" exclusively to just one religion. It is common for a Japanese person to be active in more than one religious tradition: several traditions may be combined in one religious activity, or a person may resort to one tradition for one purpose and then rely on another tradition for another purpose. For most Westerners this is difficult to understand, because in the West religion is usually a matter of exclusive affiliation: a person identifies as Protestant, Catholic, Jew, or another religious persuasion but does not participate in two, three, or more religions. How is it possible for a Japanese person to be part of so many religious traditions?

When I first began to study Japanese religion in graduate school, something that both puzzled and amazed me was its diversity. How could so many traditions coexist in the same country? And Japanese people usually have not chosen one "faith" exclusively but instead have participated in most of these traditions simultaneously or alternately. One of the reasons that I came to specialize in the study of Japanese religion was this challenge of trying to understand the unity of Japanese religion.

One cannot study Japanese religion simply by individual traditions, and then "add up" the seven or more traditions; this will not yield the "total." For Japanese religion is not a mathematical addition of individual components, it is a way of life that is constructed and supported by most of the individual components. A Japanese person does not have to "join" one religious tradition and thereby reject all others. Rather, this person comes to participate in a number of separate traditions as they form an integral part of his or her way of life. This can be illustrated for each of the seven traditions and will be seen at greater length in later chapters.

It is not necessary to formally join Shinto in order to venerate kami. Kami may be venerated daily at the household Shinto shrine (**kamidana**), or kami may be honored in seasonal festivals and as part of the rituals associated with agriculture. Any member of a family or any farmer may venerate kami as a natural part of being a family member or of farming. Similarly, it is not necessary to formally "join" Buddhism in order to worship Buddhist divinities. Such "Buddhas" may be honored daily at the household Buddhist altar (**butsudan**), or Buddhas known for granting special requests may be prayed to when one wants to make this request. Buddhist divinities are worshiped as a natural part of family devotions and in the process of resolving personal requests.

Taoism is not a separate tradition in Japan, but various "Taoistic" beliefs about the calendar and good fortune have become an integral part of the Japanese way of life. People are not "Taoists," but they rely on the calendar to choose a proper day for a wedding or funeral. Confucianism is not a separate tradition in Japan, but Confucian ideals of proper social conduct—especially loving obedience of children to parents and loyalty of citizens to rulers—have become part of Japanese thought and practice. People do not consider themselves "Confucianists" when they behave this way, but simply good children and good citizens.

Christianity is a special case, because a small number of Japanese do practice Christianity much in the same fashion as it is in the United States and Europe: they belong exclusively to Christianity and reject other traditions. But there are many more Japanese who read the Bible and draw inspiration from it without becoming members of Christian churches and without giving up other traditions.

Folk religion is so loose and informal that a person could not even think of becoming a "member." A family puts up New Year's decorations, not because it is a member of a special group, but because this is the folk custom at this time of year. Members of New Religions are in a somewhat different category, because few people participate in two or more New Religions simultaneously. But members of New Religions do participate in various other Japanese traditions. And as we shall see later, New Religions contain many traditional notions, such as the worship of kami and ancestors.

Each of these seven traditions can be considered as a separate religious line, but a better approach to understanding is to see these traditions as they fit into the pattern of religious life as it has formed and as it is practiced. When we study Japanese religion as it is acted out in daily life, most of these traditions become blended together into a unified world view of belief and action. This world view enables the Japanese to define their identity and find their place in the world, living a rich and meaningful life. Various traditions have been used as ingredients to form the total world view for a culture and a comprehensive philosophy of life for individuals. This composite world view provides the Japanese with the inspiration and spiritual power to guide them through life. In this sense we may say that Japanese religion is characterized by "many traditions within one sacred way."

What are the procedures for studying a "sacred way"? One well-known approach for studying any religious or cultural subject is to treat it historically, tracing it from its first appearance to its present form; Chapter II treats the historical formation of Japanese religion, or the sacred way. Another procedure for studying a world view is to analyze it as a total system or organization of life. In this case the focus is not on the development of parts into a whole system but on the organization of the system as a total way of life. Chapters III and IV interpret Japanese religion as a sacred way including not only objects of worship but a comprehensive understanding of the world and how to live meaningfully within it. Chapter V gives two examples that illustrate the dynamics of this sacred way as it is acted out. The final chapter looks briefly at the situation of Japanese religion today and the interaction of the modern world and the sacred way.

■

CHAPTER II

The Historical Development of Japanese Religion

One of the best ways to discover the distinctiveness of Japanese religion is to trace its emergence from diverse traditions into one national heritage. In this historical panorama, Japanese religion arises out of prehistoric practices and mixes with influences from China and India, eventually forming peculiarly Japanese institutions and practices and contributing to and being influenced by more recent changes in Japanese national life. In this chapter we will follow the historical development of Japanese religion from prehistoric times to the present. This historical overview will provide the background for understanding the organization and dynamics of Japanese religion treated in subsequent chapters.

Early Religious Customs

As we have seen in our discussion of Japanese culture, including the origin of the Japanese people and the beginnings of the Japanese language, some of the earliest aspects of Japanese life are not known to us. The origins of religious customs, too, are rather vague. In prehistoric times there were many local customs and practices, but there was no single organized religion—even Shinto did not exist as a separate tradition during this early period. Some of the prehistoric religious picture must be pieced together from archaeological information. For example, archaeologists in Japan have unearthed prehistoric female figurines and human burials within urns. From evidence such as this, they have concluded that people living in the

Japanese islands more than two thousand years ago were concerned with agricultural fertility (the female figurines were probably used in rituals related to fertility); the burials show a concern for the after-life of family members. It is difficult to trace a clear link from these prehistoric materials to the later stages of a more unified Japanese culture, but the similarities are too close to neglect. From studying the earliest written records about Japanese culture, we realize that ancient religion was closely related to both agricultural fertility and veneration of family ancestors.

The link between prehistoric evidence and later practices is illustrated also by the prehistoric remains of stone circles with a vertical pillar at the center of each circle. These stone circles may represent a kind of sun dial that also was a means of paying religious respect to the sun. According to Japanese mythological writings (*Kojiki* and *Nihongi*), the first emperor is descended from the **Sun Goddess**; even today numerous folk practices include greeting the rising sun with a prayer.

One of the most important developments of the prehistoric era was the gradual shift from a hunting and gathering economy (including fishing) to the growing of rice. This began more than two thousand years ago, and it marked the development of permanent villages and the kind of social and religious life that has been characteristic of Japan until very recent times. Rice agriculture requires a great deal of manual labor on rather small fields but yields large amounts of rice that can support a large population. This pattern of small farming villages dependent on the income from agricultural goods—especially rice—has been very important for the development of the Japanese life-style. Usually a farming family was an economic unit that worked together to till, plant, weed, and harvest. A number of these families formed small villages that cooperated in many ways—not only in agriculture and politics, but also in social events and seasonal celebrations.

The picture of religion in early Japan is not completely clear, but it seems to involve a triangle of social life organized around families, economic life centered around small farms (especially rice agriculture), and religious life concerned with family units revering the spirits of the natural world for blessings of children and bountiful crops. This is the informal, loose tradition of beliefs and practices out of which Shinto eventually emerged. The recorded prayers (norito) of ancient Shinto, which preserve the religious beliefs and practices of prehistoric times, abound with prayers for rice agriculture. To this day, the rhythm of most Shinto shrines revolves around the two key seasons of spring (when rice is transplanted) and fall (when rice is harvested). Even the all-important enthronement ceremony for a new emperor (after the death of the previous emperor) is delayed until the fall because it is patterned after the harvest festival.

From as far back as we have reliable evidence, families appear to have been unified in their worship of local kami for agricultural blessings. Apparently kami were thought to dwell within remarkable forms of nature, for example, a tall tree or a large boulder or mountain; the families of the nearby village cooperated in the celebration of seasonal festivals just as they cooperated in social life within the village and in economic life to grow rice. There was no clear membership in a specific "religion"; in fact, probably there was no clear conception of "religion" apart from social and economic life: all aspects of life must have blended together.

This interaction of social, economic, and religious life gradually developed into a more complex cultural pattern, with some families owning more land and controlling more wealth. About the beginning of the Christian era, when Japanese culture was becoming more complex, the influence of continental Asian culture entered Japan by way of Korea. This new influence included advancements such as metal crafts, armed horsemen, and elaborate burial mausoleums (reserved for leading families). Gradually this pattern of social, economic, and religious life developed into a more highly centralized and organized national identity that has come to be known as Japan. One of the key features of the emerging national identity was the respect paid to one leading family as the imperial line of the national heritage. The traditional accounts of the origin of the imperial line are recorded in some of the earliest written documents, the *Kojiki* and *Nihongi*. These writings begin with a mythological account of the creation of Japan and then describe legendary emperors and chronicles historical emperors. A brief summary of the mythological parts of these documents helps us better understand traditional Japanese notions about the creation of Japan and the sacred origin of the imperial line.

The *Kojiki* and *Nihongi*, completed in the early eighth century but recording myths and legends much older, give a similar account of the "age of the kami," when creation took place. According to these records, "At the time of the beginning of heaven and earth," there came into existence many kami. The world was not completely formed—a mixture of water and land—and the various kami produced other kami, eventually giving rise to a divine couple, Izanagi and his spouse, Izanami. Looking down from heaven on the still unformed earth, they dipped a jeweled spear into the ocean, and from this action the first islands—solid land—were formed. This is the mythological precedent for the sacred character of the Japanese islands as created by kami.

The divine couple gave birth to other mythological figures, the most important of whom is the Sun Goddess (**Amaterasu**). Later the Sun Goddess ordered her grandson, Ninigi, to descend to earth and rule it; as signs of this right to rule, she gave him a necklace, a mirror, and a sword. These three objects are still respected today as the symbols of imperial power. According to Japanese tradition, the subsequent emperors of Japan down to the present emperor constitute an unbroken line of hereditary descendants from these divine parents. This is the mythological background for the sacred character of the Japanese emperor as descended from these central kami. Even the Japanese people are thought to be descended indirectly from kami, making them a sacred people distinct from other people.

These mythological accounts show us that from early times there was a clear notion of Japan as a divine country led by a sacred emperor and inhabited by a people who had a special relationship to kami. This early combination of sacred origin for the Japanese islands, the emperor, and the Japanese people provided the foundation for a distinctively Japanese religious tradition. In Japan, as in any tradition, the interpretation of such mythological origins has ranged from a completely literal to a rather figurative interpretation. Most Japanese today do not hold a completely literal view of their sacred origins. However, unconsciously the notion of the land, people, and culture of Japan as a distinctive tradition persists—and the emperor remains the symbolic head of the nation. These early Japanese beliefs and practices formed the background for the development of a more highly organized religious heritage in connection with "foreign" traditions.

Chinese and Indian Influence

The history of Japanese religion begins with the informal tradition of customs, beliefs, and practices from prehistoric Japan, but Japanese religion formed and developed in close relationship with influences from relatively nearby China and distant India. One of the crucial events in Japanese history was the introduction of Chinese culture, starting from about the sixth century A.D. Prior to this time, Japanese culture was not highly developed—there was no written language, little graphic art, no complex philosophical systems, and no government unified around a central state. Chinese culture was abundantly rich in all of these: a sophisticated writing system (including poetry and literature); elaborate art forms, especially painting (and thanks to Buddhism, magnificent statues); grand philosophical systems; and highly efficient governmental structures. it was only natural for Japan to adopt and adapt much of Chinese culture and religion at a time when Japanese forms of culture and government were becoming more highly organized. This is not to say that Japan "borrowed" everything and does not have a distinct culture of its own. It may be more appropriate to say that China is a cultural watershed for Japan, much as Greece and Rome are a cultural resource for Europe and America.

China has been a transmitter, not only of native Chinese culture, but also of distant Indian culture. Buddhism, which was founded in India in the sixth century B.C. by the Buddha, was introduced to China about the time of the Christian era and became increasingly influential. Buddhism had already become part of Chinese culture when, several centuries later, both were formally transmitted to Japan. The formal introduction of Buddhism into Japan occurred in the sixth century A.D., when a ruler from a Korean kingdom solicited military help from Japan and included Buddhist writings and statues as part of his tribute. According to the account in the *Nihongi*, at first the Japanese were afraid to worship these Buddhist statues, fearing that native kami would be jealous of "foreign kami." But they did worship the Buddhas, and when an epidemic broke out, it was considered a bad omen. Therefore, the statues were thrown away, until another omen showed that the epidemic was not due to the acceptance of Buddhism, and the Buddhist statues were worshiped once more.

This early incident is significant for understanding the development of Japanese religion. For one thing, foreign religions such as Buddhism were accepted for the power and blessings they were able to grant. Later, more abstract and philosophical aspects of Buddhism were interpreted by scholars, but to this day one of the major attractions of Buddhism is its power to provide blessings to people in their daily life. Another important aspect of this incident is that acceptance of Buddhas and Buddhism did not mean rejection of the native religion and kami. Rather, both Buddhas and kami were worshiped, often side by side. This is a good example of the kind of interaction among religious traditions that is so important in the development, organization, and dynamics of Japanese religion.

Chinese culture had its impact on almost every aspect of Japanese culture, and in every instance when Chinese elements were "borrowed," they were also modified to fit Japanese culture. As we have seen with Japanese language, Chinese writing forms were used to write the Japanese language, but Japanese language retained its grammatical structure and used special phonetic signs to link the written Chinese characters. The written and spoken forms of Chinese and Japanese differ considerably, with Japanese retaining its own characteristics. China was the grand model to be followed in many plans of developing Japan. Even Japan's first permanent capital city, Nara (established in 710), was laid out after the fashion of the Chinese capital at the time. The governmental bureaucracies and systems of ranks for people were adopted from Chinese precedents. Later these Chinese patterns were modified or even abandoned, but the stamp of Chinese culture had been permanently imprinted on the Japanese scene.

Two examples of religious and philosophical influence from China are Confucianism and Taoism. Confucianism emphasized the principle of social harmony through a set of hierarchical relationships in which the subordinate person (such as a son) is obedient and loyal, the higher person (such as a father) is benevolent and protective. In Japan, family units and social cooperation had been important before the introduction of Confucianism, but the new teaching provided a systematic means of reinforcing family loyalty, cooperation among groups, and even support for the state. Respect for the emperor as head of the leading family was further stimulated by the Confucian teaching of loyalty of subjects to rulers. The Japanese imperial tradition differed from the Chinese imperial system in one fundamental sense, however. The Japanese imperial line had the right to rule by hereditary descent from the founding kami; the Chinese imperial system was based on a "mandate of heaven" according to which heaven not only selected emperors but also could remove bad emperors (against whom the country might rebel). On this fundamental issue, the Japanese retained their traditional notion, rejecting the Chinese notion that could shift leadership from one family to another. In this case, as in other instances, Japan adopted a "both-and" stance, *both* accepting the Chinese Confucian notion to reinforce the authority of the emperor *and* retaining the Japanese tradition of the imperial line's traditional descent from the kami.

Taoism's influence in Japan was first formalized in the Bureau of Divination (Onmyoryo), which the government adopted after the Chinese bureaucratic model. This bureau was the official means of incorporating Taoistic practices into the government. The Bureau of Divination, in Japan as in China, had as its major task the determining of auspicious timing for governmental events and the interpretation of good and bad omens appearing in nature (especially unusual phenomena). The Bureau of Divination was adopted in the early eighth century, when the Japanese government was being remodeled after Chinese patterns.

In the case of Taoism, too, there were earlier Japanese notions and practices that made it easy to accept the basic principles of the new tradition. The prehistoric Japanese heritage of veneration for nature and the many kami inhabiting the natural world formed a receptive context for Taoism, with its emphasis on harmony with nature. Even if the Japanese did not have a philosophical system to express it in abstract principles, they were actually living out a way of nature in their worship of the kami. Gradually Taoism became part of the Japanese religious heritage. The Chinese calendar taken from Taoist practice filtered into both Shinto and Buddhism. Popular practitioners (*hijiri*) of Taoistic techniques wandered among the people and spread these teachings throughout the country. Eventually Taoist beliefs and practices became so thoroughly "Japanized" that most Japanese people would have difficulty identifying Taoist features within Japanese religion.

Although India is a continent away from the Japanese islands, and even though it was a long time before any Japanese traveled to India, nevertheless the Indian religion of Buddhism made a greater impact on the Japanese tradition than any other foreign religion. We have already seen that Buddhism, a religion founded in sixth century B.C. India as a teaching of enlightenment, was first transformed within Chinese culture and then brought through Korea to Japan about the sixth century A.D. When Buddhism entered Japan, it brought more than just the basic philosophy of enlightenment: it included powerful magical rituals and rites for ancestors and the prosperity of the nation, as well as elaborate art forms such as statues. When Buddhism was accepted in Japan, it was more than just a set of principles or a religious faith—it was part of a total way of life or civilization. The many facets of Buddhism were first accepted in Japan by the imperial family and the nobility at court.

From the start of its successful career in Japan, Buddhism was viewed as a powerful means of obtaining practical benefits in association with native kami. Quickly the power of Buddhist divinities was associated with the imperial line and kami. Buddhism became so much a part of life at the court that it even provided rituals for safe childbirth for the empress, as well as other healing rituals. By the early eighth century, a Buddhist priest and an empress had set the Japanese precedent for having their bodies cremated, following Buddhist ritual. Buddhist memorial rites for the dead became important for the court.

In the eighth century, an emperor ordered the building of a kind of national cathedral for Buddhism, housing a large statue of the Sun Buddha. According to tradition, messengers were sent to the most important of all Shinto shrines, Ise, to consult the oracle there about the propriety of erecting this statue of the Sun Buddha. The answer was that the Sun Buddha and the Sun Goddess (enshrined at Ise) were identical. This shows how Buddhism rapidly entered the life of Shinto and the nation. At about the same time as the building of this great cathedral, every province in Japan was ordered to build a monastery and a nunnery, where monks and nuns studied Buddhist scriptures and performed rites for the sake of the nation.

Buddhism was patronized by emperors personally and by the state as a matter of policy. Some of the imperial court may have been attracted to the more doctrinal and philosophical aspects of Buddhism, but the majority of the court and nobility were drawn directly to the ritual power and aesthetic richness of Buddhism. State support for Buddhism enhanced the role of the emperor as an enlightened Buddhist ruler and helped ensure a peaceful and prosperous reign. Because the state used Buddhism partly as a means to reinforce its rule, it did not encourage the spread of Buddhism to the people. (In fact, at this time the state prohibited the teaching of Buddhism to the masses.) In this early period Buddhism existed mainly among the court and nobility. A variety of philosophical teachings from Indian Buddhism were transmitted to Japan in Chinese translation, but development of a distinctively Japanese Buddhism and its spread to the people came later.

Chinese and Indian religion made a permanent impact on Japanese religion through various influences—Taoism, Confucianism, and Buddhism. However, Japanese religion has retained a distinctive tradition, based on the prehistoric heritage and Shinto, and has influenced the "foreign" traditions accepted in Japan.

The Flowering of Japanese Buddhism

One of the remarkable features in Japanese religious history is the rapid development and extensive spread of Buddhism. The career of Buddhism in Japan is an interesting example of the power and flexibility of Buddhism and the adaptive and innovative character of Japanese culture. Indian Buddhism possessed a wide variety of doctrine and ritual, which was further enriched by its relationship to each new culture it encountered. China, Korea, and Japan accepted and transmitted Buddhist teachings and practices, and in the process, each country adapted Buddhism to its particular culture. Buddhism flowered in Japan especially from the ninth to the fourteenth century, developing the sects that have attracted the largest numbers of followers from that time to the present.

This expansion of Buddhism occurred especially during two major periods of Japanese history, the Heian (794–1185) and the Kamakura (1185–1333). During the Heian period, Japanese culture began to absorb and refine in a more independent fashion the heritage accepted from China. Early in the Heian period, two great Japanese Buddhists founded their own sects, each patterned after Chinese models but also formed in close relationship to Japanese culture. These two founders, Kukai (774–835, known posthumously as Kobo Daishi) and Saicho (762–822, known posthumously as Dengyo Daishi), went to China to bring back to Japan a more authentic Buddhism. Kukai was most attracted to the Chinese form of Buddhism known as Chen-yen (**Shingon**, in Japanese), whereas Saicho was drawn to the Chinese form of T'ien-t'ai (**Tendai**, in Japanese).

Chen-yen Buddhism is the Chinese form of esoteric Buddhism transmitted from India. (A similar form of esoteric Buddhism was transmitted from India to Tibet.) It is called esoteric because it focuses on complicated doctrines, rituals, and paintings as the means for gaining enlightenment, that is, realizing these esoteric truths in one's own life. Kukai brought back from China especially the Buddhist scriptures (in Chinese translation), ritual tools, and secret teachings that conveyed this esoteric realization of Buddhism. Kukai founded his new Buddhist sect, Shingon, on remote Mount Koya, partly in order to separate his new Buddhism from the older Buddhist schools at the former capital of Nara. He also stressed blending Buddhism with native practices and venerated the local kami of the mountain together with Buddhist deities. Esoteric Buddhism caught on rapidly at the court, especially because of its elaborate rituals (such as a fire ritual, for example). The impressive statues and mysterious magical formulas transmitted by Shingon Buddhism have become part of Japanese culture generally, accepted by most people whether or not they belong to the Shingon sect. Kukai is fondly remembered by the Japanese as an important literary figure, and he is the hero of many traditional folk tales.

Saicho brought back from China the T'ien-t'ai form of Buddhism and continued most of its practices in the Tendai sect he founded in Japan. Tendai Buddhism is based especially on the Lotus Sutra, using its teachings to draw all other aspects of Buddhism together into a grand vision of the unity of all existence. The Lotus Sutra, one of the most widely known Buddhist scriptures in east Asia, is popular among the common people for its easily understood parables, illustrating that every person can attain enlightenment through simple acts of devotion. Another aspect of Tendai practice is faith in the Buddhist divinity named Amida and meditation on Amida or recitation of faith in Amida as an act of piety. Saicho set up his sect headquarters on Mount Hiei, near Kyoto, the new capital (moved there from Nara in 794). He developed close ties with the faith and practice of kami on this mountain, which he established as a center of meditation and study. This sect and its mountain headquarters were extremely important as sources of inspiration for other sects that spread and popularized Buddhism.

In the Kamakura period (1185–1333), power shifted from the imperial court and nobility to a military dictator and warriors located at Kamakura. As feudal lords fought to control and conquer territory, there was widespread warfare and an atmosphere of uncertainty that influenced the entire culture, even religion. The three new sects founded during the Kamakura period helped resolve the sense of uncertainty, providing simpler techniques of faith and practice and making direct contact with the common people. These three new sects are the **Pure Land**, Nichiren, and Zen. The founders of these sects had studied at the Tendai headquarters on Mount Hiei but developed different strands of Buddhism into major sects.

The Pure Land tradition in Buddhism was developed in China as the practice of faith in the Buddhist divinity Amitabha (Amida, in Japanese), which enabled a person to be reborn in the heavenly paradise, or pure land, of this Buddhist divinity. This faith was present in Japan earlier, but not until Honen (1133–1212) made it the basis of his teaching did it become a separate tradition. Honen stressed faith in Amida and preached to the masses this very simple means of using Buddhist power to be reborn in the pure land (somewhat different from other notions of "enlightenment"). The exact form of this recitation, *namu Amida Butsu* ("I place my faith in Amida Buddha"), is so short that anyone can recite it, even while working. Later there were disagreements among Pure Land leaders about whether the essence of this recitation's power was in its constant repetition, or in the total faith of just one recitation. But in spite of these theoretical differences, faith in Amida became very popular among the common people.

The denominations of the Pure Land developed strong parish organizations, and Pure Land priests are credited with setting the precedent of a married Buddhist priesthood. (Formerly, there was a celibate priesthood.) This was important for the development of "household Buddhism" in Japan, a pattern in which all sects eventually accepted the custom of married Buddhist priests controlling local temples (almost like family businesses). The influence of the Japanese family is reflected in this development of "household Buddhism."

The Nichiren sect is named after the man Nichiren (1222–1281), one of the most forceful personalities in all Japanese religious history. He concentrated on the Lotus Sutra as the embodiment of absolute truth and lived his life according to it. He rejected all other forms of Buddhism and called for the state to eliminate them, in order to establish the state on the foundation of the true Buddhism of the Lotus Sutra. Nichiren's technique for practicing faith in the Lotus Sutra was to recite *namu Myoho Rengekyo* ("I place my faith in the Lotus Sutra"). This enabled every person to resolve any worldly problem, benefiting not only the individual, but also the Japanese state. The denominations of Nichiren Buddhism are the most nationalistic of all Japanese Buddhist groups, a good example of how the universal message of Buddhism can be made into a highly particular national expression. Nichiren faith is exclusivistic (rejecting all other forms of Buddhism), and Nichiren's aggressive missionary style (sometimes compared to the Salvation Army in the West) has been an important model for recently developed New Religions (such as Soka Gakkai).

Zen is a form of Buddhism emphasizing meditation that developed in China into a separate tradition (called Ch'an in Chinese). Some Buddhist meditation had been practiced in Japan earlier, but not until Eisai (1141–1215) and Dogen (1200–1253) made their trips to China was Zen practiced in Japan as a separate tradition. Zen claims to be the continuation of the meditation practiced by the Buddha to gain enlightenment, but it was also influenced by Taoist ideals (such as the love of nature) and developed in China into highly formal meditation techniques. In formal Zen meditation, monks sit in a special hall for a number of hours each day, continuing this practice for months or even years until each monk is enlightened. Eisai and Dogen each brought back a particular form of this meditation. Zen priests also brought refined Chinese culture to Japan, which helped attract members of the ruling class to Zen as much as the meditation practices did. Gradually, the strict meditation of Zen, mixed with other devotional practices and memorial rites, attracted members of the warrior class. Zen's acceptance by the common people was made possible especially by Zen providing practical memorial rites for the family. In Japan the notion of sudden enlightenment blended with the Japanese love of nature so well that Zen teaching of enlightenment, or awakening, was interpreted as knowing one's own heart and being in tune with nature. The insights of Zen as a way of life have penetrated Japanese culture so thoroughly—from the fine arts to the martial arts—that it is sometimes identified with the spirit of Japan. In the present century, Zen has become popular in the West as a means of disciplining the body and mind to a more enlightened, peaceful way of life.

These new Buddhist sects, from Shingon and Tendai in the Heian period to the Pure Land, Nichiren, and Zen in the Kamakura period, are solid evidence of the extent to which Japanese religion has been influenced by Buddhism. However, the process by which these sects were accepted also shows the features of Japanese culture that made it possible to accept foreign traditions and mold them to Japanese custom. Whenever Japan has borrowed, the result has been both adoption and adaptation. Buddhism once was a "foreign" religion for Japan, but it quickly became naturalized as "Japanese Buddhism."

Medieval Religion

From the fourteenth through the eighteenth centuries, Japanese religion continued to develop in a number of ways. Buddhist sects split into competing denominations and spread throughout most of Japan. Shinto shrines became more highly organized and came to develop more systematic teachings in reaction to Buddhism. Toward the end of this medieval period, Christianity, another "foreign" tradition, entered Japan and enjoyed brief success before it was banned. A strong feudal society emerged with a comprehensive Confucian rationale.

Shinto grew out of the native tradition of early Japanese religion, especially the beliefs and practices related to the kami, but Shinto also freely accepted Chinese and Buddhist influences. Eventually Shinto incorporated ethical notions from Confucianism, a religious calendar and associated beliefs from Taoism, and philosophical systems and ritual practices from Buddhism. As with other Japanese borrowing, Shinto retained its original character but added these "foreign" elements, creating a more complex tradition.

Buddhism was the most prominent influence incorporated by Shinto, on both the theoretical and the practical levels. The best example of Buddhist influence on the theoretical level is the idea of Buddhist divinities and kami as counterparts, almost as if the two were opposite sides of the same coin. Throughout Southeast Asia as well as East Asia, Buddhism tended to blend with other religions and honor local deities (rather than rejecting the other religions and replacing local deities with Buddhist divinities). Japanese Buddhist scholars used a Chinese Buddhist theory to develop their notion that Buddhist divinities represent the original substance of reality, whereas kami represent the worldly "trace" or counterpart of the original substance. In this theory, Buddhist scholars valued Buddhist divinities as the primary or higher reality. However, as Shinto scholars began to form their own systems of thought, borrowing from other traditions, they began to assert the primary value of Shinto. One change Shinto scholars made was to reverse the counterpart theory, claiming that kami represent the original substance of reality and Buddhist divinities the worldly "trace" or counterpart of kami. This was an important precedent for Shinto priests and scholars in beginning to reclaim their position in Japanese religion and society.

For most people the interaction of Shinto and Buddhism was more important at the concrete level in local Shinto shrines. The interaction was so complete that Shinto shrines enshrined both Buddhist divinities and kami, and Buddhist temples and Shinto shrines were built next to each other as part of the same religious center. The common people prayed to both kami and Buddhist divinities and did not seem to concern themselves with the subtle differences between the Shinto and the Buddhist versions of the counterpart theory. These religions became interrelated to the point that Shinto prayers (norito) were read before Buddhist divinities and Buddhist scriptures were read before Shinto kami. This pattern of interrelated Shinto and Buddhist practices was transmitted to distant areas of Japan as Shinto shrines were built there. Sometimes the same priest served in both Shinto and Buddhist capacities, although generally Buddhist priests held more powerful positions. Gradually Shinto priests and scholars began to work for a stronger role for Shinto in the life of the nation.

The blending of Buddhism with Shinto shows how a foreign tradition gradually became naturalized as a Japanese tradition. Christianity first entered Japan much later than Buddhism and up to the present is still considered by most Japanese to be a foreign religion. Saint Francis Xavier first brought Christianity (Roman Catholicism) to Japan in 1549, arriving on Portuguese trade ships. In spite of the basic differences between Catholic Christianity and Japanese religion, Christianity experienced a brief but remarkable success before it was suppressed about a hundred years later. This "Christian century" is a good example of the meeting of two different cultures and religions.

The basic principles of belief and practice are quite different for Christianity and Japanese religion. Christianity is based on faith and worship of one true God, whereas Japanese religion is based on belief in and worship of both local kami (gods) and various Buddhist divinities. Christianity claims the exclusive attention of believers, not allowing participation in another religion; in Japanese religion, the usual practice is for a person (or family) to participate in several religious traditions. These and other differences between the two traditions made it unlikely that Catholicism would succeed in Japan, but the Catholic missionaries overcame these differences to convert a number of the Japanese in a relatively short time.

One political factor that initially helped Catholicism gain support was the government's attempt to limit the power of Buddhist organizations (such as the monasteries on Mount Hiei): the state apparently allowed Christian missions into Japan in order to offset Buddhist strength. Eventually the government gained complete control over Buddhism and began to suspect political motives of the Catholic missionaries, all of whom came from Europe. The Japanese rulers also feared that if Japanese Christians were loyal to the foreign Catholic priests and a foreign God, they might side with Europeans against Japan in a war. Early in the seventeenth century, the government began to move against Christianity and by 1640 had almost totally eliminated Christian missionaries and Christianity from the Japanese islands.

The total ban on Christianity was enforced with policies that had a lasting effect on the organization of Japanese religion. In order to make sure that no Christians remained in Japan, the government required every family to belong to a local Buddhist temple and report all births, marriages, deaths, and changes of address to this temple. Family affiliation with a Buddhist temple became a hereditary custom: funeral and memorial rites for family members were performed by a local Buddhist temple. This set the pattern for hereditary family affiliation to local parish Buddhist temples.

It was the Tokugawa family line of military rulers that unified Japan in a form of feudal order, gaining control over the powerful Buddhist temples and then suppressing Christianity. The Tokugawa period (1600–1867) was a time of centralization of power and stability, with foreign influence excluded. The feudal order, headed by the Tokugawa family, controlled most aspects of life and used the local Buddhist temple almost like a census office to register families.

The Tokugawa government also relied heavily on the rationale of Confucian teachings to support a hierarchical society with four classes: warriors were the highest class, followed by farmers, then workers, and, in the lowest position, merchants. Warriors were considered highest because they protected the state, and farmers were relatively high in position because they produced the wealth (such as rice and other agricultural goods) that supported the society. Workers were next because they did provide services; merchants were lowest because they simply lived on the profit of others and did not produce any wealth or service. Some of the basic assumptions of the Confucian thought behind this system are an economy based on agriculture, a hierarchical society with little movement from class to class, and the duty of all to work within their respective classes for the good of the entire society. Loyalty to superiors and to the state was stressed. Although some of these ideas originated with Confucius and later followers, they blended with Japanese notions of life and morality.

During Tokugawa times a comprehensive philosophy of life took shape in which people felt indebted for the blessings of nature and kami, expressed gratitude to parents and ancestors for the gift of life, and were loyal toward their political superiors. As in any social or political system, there were abuses, and occasionally the farmers and townspeople protested against unfair policies. But the occasional protests did not seek a revolution to overturn the government and reject this comprehensive philosophy of life. There have been many changes in Japan since Tokugawa times (which ended in 1867), but many of the values developed during the Tokugawa period still influence Japanese life today.

Religion Enters the Modern World

There are two major turning points that separate traditional Japan from modern Japan and traditional Japanese religion from modern Japanese religion. The first is the end of the feudal government in 1867 and the beginning of a national government in the Meiji period (1868–1911); the second is the end of World War II in 1945 and the blossoming of many democratic freedoms. Religion helped bring about these dramatic changes, and in turn was affected by the changes.

The Meiji era marks the end of the more than two hundred years of Japan's relative isolation from the rest of the world during Tokugawa times. Due to changing internal conditions (especially the dominance of commerce over agriculture), the feudal system of government weakened, and foreign powers increasingly demanded the opening of Japan to trade. In the end, the feudal government was abolished and replaced with a national government symbolically headed by the emperor; power was held by a form of parliamentary government. One aspect of this change in government was the opening of Japan to political and commercial relations with other countries.

A main support for this new government was Shinto, which for centuries had been trying to reassert itself as a central factor in national life. From medieval times, Shinto had claimed that the worship of kami (rather than the "foreign" Buddhism) was the true national heritage of Japan, and that the emperor (rather than the military ruler) was the true ruler of Japan. Even study of the Chinese tradition of Confucianism, through its encouragement of scholarship on classical literature, promoted study of the ancient Japanese writings *Kojiki* and *Nihongi*, as well as Japanese mythological and historical writings honored within Shinto. In this complex sequence of events leading out of feudal times and into the modern age, Shinto was a force that helped bring about the formation of the new government in 1868 and influenced government policies in the following decades.

In the development of a national form of government, feudal forms were abolished: feudal lords, feudal territories, feudal armies, and the feudal class system. Henceforth, people were considered citizens of Japan as a nation, and national institutions were set up: national taxes, a national army, provinces (similar to states) under a national government, and a national parliament and cabinet holding actual power. The general effect of these changes was to harm Buddhism (which had been identified with the feudal government) and to benefit Shinto (which had supported the change in government and the greater role of the empire).

Families were no longer required to belong to Buddhist temples, and there was some persecution of Buddhist temples. But Buddhism was so close to the hearts of the people that the persecution quickly died out. Part of the rationale for forming a new government was to "restore" the emperor as the true ruler and Shinto as the true national heritage, but it was difficult to implement these ideals in actual practice. The emperor was a very important symbol around which the nation could be unified, but he held little actual power. Although there were many attempts to make Shinto a central feature of the government, eventually Shinto was used more as a patriotic rationale than as an established religion.

One factor that helped bring about relative freedom of religion was the effect of the government's policies toward Christianity. At the beginning of the Meiji era in 1868, when the ban on Christianity had not been lifted, it was discovered that some Japanese families had secretly continued their practice of Christianity for two hundred years. These "hidden Christians" were severely punished by the Japanese government, and this news traveled rapidly to Western countries. When representatives of the Japanese government toured Western countries in order to study modern social and political conditions in these countries and develop better ties with them, they encountered hostility because of the recent suppression of hidden Christians. This helped persuade the government to remove the ban on Christianity in 1873; in 1889, the Meiji constitution formally gave Japanese citizens relative freedom of religion "within limits not prejudicial to peace and order, and not antagonistic to their duties as subjects." However, until 1945 this formal freedom of religion was severely restricted by government and police. The change in government policy did allow Christianity to officially re-enter Japan, through both Catholic and (for the first time) Protestant missionaries. Christianity gained a small number of converts and made some important contributions to Japanese society, especially in education and social welfare. But from about 1890, with the heightened nationalism accompanying the Sino-Japanese war (1894–95) and the Russo-Japanese War (1904–5), the Japanese turned more to their native traditions and did not enter Christianity in significant numbers.

Japanese society changed rapidly during the Meiji era (1868–1911), and even during the late Tokugawa times (1600–1867), some new religious movements had appeared. During Meiji and thereafter, other New Religions appeared, and all these movements continued to attract followers in spite of government efforts to hinder and suppress them. From the 1920s through the end of World War II in 1945, Japanese society and politics were increasingly dominated by nationalism, and the same held true for Japanese religion. Although the Meiji constitution officially granted freedom of religion, actual government policies made it difficult to practice religion freely.

The state had declared Shinto to be "nonreligious," in the sense that it was the patriotic duty of all Japanese as citizens of the state to pay their respects at Shinto shrines (honoring the foundation of the country); schoolchildren, for example, were required to visit and "pay respects" at Shinto shrines. Many Shinto shrines and Shinto priests were directly subsidized by the state. There was a law against teaching "religion" (such as Buddhism or Christianity) in the schools; but "national ethics" was required—a mixture of Shinto and Confucian teachings about the sacred character of the Japanese nation and Japanese people by virtue of their creation by the kami and the ethical responsibility of the people to be loyal to the emperor and the state. These teachings helped unify the country and mobilize it for war before and during World War II. Shinto was at the forefront of this effort, but there was remarkable unity in the support for national and military goals by Shinto, Buddhism, and even Japanese Christianity.

The end of World War II in 1945 marked not only the defeat of Japan and a disruption of the national government, but also considerable change for Japanese religion. The Allied Occupation of 1945–52, led by the United States, helped establish a new constitution, with greater political and individual freedom and complete freedom of religion. Shinto had been disestablished; formally, the government could neither favor nor discriminate against any religion, and indirectly the compulsory teaching (or indoctrination) of "national ethics" was stopped. All religions were allowed to exist freely (including Shinto), supported by voluntary membership, with no coerced attendance, and no financial subsidy from the state. However, the principle of separation of church and state is a delicate issue in many modern countries, and there are still unresolved issues in Japan today. For example, the emperor is a symbolic figure representing the nation; his involvement in key Shinto rituals has been interpreted as a "private" affair, but because he receives money from the state, does this mean that the state indirectly helps finance these rituals?

Two other examples of the problem of the separation of religion and the state are the Ise Shrine and the Yasukuni Shrine. The Ise Shrine is considered the most important Shinto shrine for the Japanese nation as a whole, because tradition holds that the Sun Goddess (from whom the imperial line descends) is enshrined there. The Yasukuni Shrine is a special shrine in Tokyo for the war dead. After World War II, government subsidy of these shrines was stopped, on the grounds that the new constitution prohibits the establishment of any religion or the financial support of any religion. But many people seek to change the constitution, arguing that these shrines represent national traditions and qualify for national support (like the Tomb of the Unknown Soldier in Arlington, Virginia); others think that if the government renews financial support for these Shinto shrines, it could also renew the nationalism and militarism that led to Japan's involvement in World War II. These issues still generate heated discussion.

Shinto suffered most from the people's demoralization after defeat in World War II. Many people stopped attending and contributing to Shinto shrines. Some of Shinto's problems were the result of gradual changes over the past century, such as the move away from a rural, agricultural life-style to a more urban, industrial life-style and greater concern for economic and "secular" matters. These changes, and the high degree of social mobility that accompanied them, were forces that tended to shift people away from participating in the seasonal festivals and local shrines of Shinto. Nevertheless, Shinto lives on in the hearts of many people as a continuation of the belief in kami, the celebration of seasonal festivals and city festivals, and a general blessing for the Japanese people.

Buddhism, too, had supported the war effort, but people did not link it so closely to war and defeat as they did Shinto. Also, Buddhism was not affected so much by social mobility. Buddhism's financial foundation was more secure, because it was based mainly on the fees for funerals and memorial rites for ancestors through hereditary affiliation. More families retained the hereditary family connection to a parish Buddhist temple than to participation in a local Shinto shrine (where affiliation traditionally was to the shrine near the family residence). A similar pattern held true for the home, especially in city apartments: the tendency was for families not to install Shinto-style altars but to retain Buddhist-style altars for family ancestors. One reason for retaining Buddhist altars has been the strong sense of family loyalty, which is expressed through veneration of ancestors at the Buddhist altar in the home. In addition, both large Buddhist temples and Shinto shrines with income from rented land were hurt by the government's postwar land reform, which distributed the large holdings of landlords (including temples and shrines) to tenants.

Christianity suffered severely from the war, because most Christians and Christian churches were located in cities and thus felt directly the death and destruction of bombing focused on cities. There was some rise in church membership after World War II, but Christians (baptized members) still represent less than one percent of the Japanese population.

One of the main results of the complete religious freedom after World War II has been the flourishing of many New Religions (such as Tenrikyo and Soka Gakkai), which had been suppressed and persecuted before 1945. Hundreds, even thousands, of these movements sprang up: some died out; some remained small; some grew in membership to hundreds of thousands, or even millions. Today Japan is a mixture of old and new. Some of the old traditions, like the belief in kami, go back to ancient times; others, like the New Religions, are relatively new. (In the final chapter we will consider the significant changes in Japanese religion throughout history and their implications for the prospects of religion in contemporary Japan.)

This historical overview of Japanese religion shows us the manner in which many traditions emerged, took shape, and interacted to form "'one sacred way." Tracing the course of religion's development in Japan, we recognize both continuity and discontinuity within the historical panorama of this sacred way: for example, in the history of beliefs and practices related to the kami, contemporary practices are continuous with those of prehistoric times, and yet they have been blended with other traditions, such as Buddhism. The course of Buddhism, too, represents both continuity and discontinuity. When Buddhism entered Japan it was a foreign religion encountering the native Japanese culture, and therefore a kind of discontinuity; but as it was adapted to Japanese culture (providing blessings for the state and memorial rituals for family ancestors) it came to form a continuity with the Japanese heritage.

This historical overview also helps us to pinpoint the general features shared with other religions and the features more distinctive of Japanese religion. For example, throughout the world, religion is concerned with purification and rituals for the dead, and Japanese religion shares this concern. But in Japan beliefs and rituals related to purification and the dead are raised to a much higher level of importance. In Japan purification is more than just a preparation for other rituals, it is practically a sacred state; the dead members of a family are so highly valued that they are honored as sacred sources of power. This is one of the distinctive aspects of the Japanese religious tradition we have discovered in tracing its historical development. To view the distinctive character of the "sacred way" more directly, we will shift from the historical perspective of the present chapter to a perspective that sees Japanese religion's unified world view in the next chapter.

CHAPTER III

The World of Worship

There are so many aspects to religion, and religious life is so closely related to other areas of life, that a number of approaches can be used to study a particular religious tradition. The philosophical aspect of religious thought can be treated separately, for example. Or the relation of religious life to social conditions and psychological states can be taken as a special area of investigation. But these specialized approaches are by their very nature limited; they tend to focus on just one aspect of a religion or on the relationships of religious life to other areas of life rather than the nature of a religion as a distinct tradition. If we set aside these specialized approaches and look at the nature of a religious heritage as a whole tradition, there are basically two possible perspectives: studying a religion from the viewpoint of its historical development, and studying it as a unified world view. The historical perspective is so widely used and well known that it needs little explanation. As seen in the last chapter, the historical approach traces a subject (the life of a person, the course of a nation, or the development of a religion) from its earliest beginnings through its various changes to its present form. Studying religion as a world view is not so widely understood and thus requires some explanation.

Studying Religion as a World View

In contrast to the historical perspective that studies a subject as it occurs or develops through time, approaching the subject as a world view means to study it as a unified system *apart* from its development through time. In other words, historical study traces how something continues and changes through time, whereas the focus on world view examines the nature of a person, nation, or religion at any given moment. From this perspective, a person is studied not in terms of chronological development but as a whole person or organized personality, in terms of major ideas and practices that are expressed by the mature person. In fact, a person can be considered as a "world," in the sense of a world of ideas or an artistic world—for example, the world of Shakespeare, or the world of Beethoven. A culture is studied from the perspective of world view, not in terms of historical development, but through the overall pattern of ideals and practices that are characteristic of this culture. For example, "the classical world," or "the world of ancient Greece," refers to the entire world or civilization of an age or culture. Similarly, a religion is studied as a world view, not by tracing its gradual growth, but by interpreting it as an interrelated system of distinctive beliefs and practices. The world view approach, like the historical perspective, can be used to study almost any human or cultural subject.

There are disagreements about exactly how these two approaches are best used, but it is obvious that some balance between the two is necessary. We cannot trace historical development through time unless we have some notion of the totality of the system we are tracing. And we cannot analyze the unity of a system without some idea of how that unity took shape. The balance between these two approaches becomes apparent from the biological example of studying an oak tree. The developmental or "historical" study of an oak follows the growth of an acorn into a seedling and sapling until the mature tree is formed. An oak can also be studied as a mature, unified form constituting a world of its own. This kind of study examines a cross section of the oak, analyzing such features as the layers of bark, the rings of the tree, and the characteristics of the wood. This helps determine the nature of an oak tree, as distinguished from tracing its development. These are two different ways of looking at the same tree: both are needed for a more complete understanding of the oak tree. The same kind of balance is necessary for the successful study of religion and other human subjects. To simplify matters, I have called these two approaches historical development and world view.

To study religion as a world view is to focus on the basic pattern of beliefs and practices that is distinctive for a religion. For example, in Europe and America, religion is centered around the belief and worship of God, especially as practiced in regular services at local churches and synagogues attended by individuals and families. This is only a quick glimpse of the nature or "world" of European and American religion, but it illustrates what is meant by looking at religion as a world view. And, by contrast, we know from the previous chapters that this pattern is quite different from the pattern of Japanese religion.

To discuss Japanese religion as a world view, it is essential to specify the religion of a general time span. For the purposes of this treatment, we will concentrate more on recent and modern religion, from the late Tokugawa period (about 1800) to the present. As shown in Chapter II, during the Tokugawa period the various traditions interacted to form a definitive heritage that continues—with modifications—even today. Where necessary, differences in religious belief and practice over this range of several hundred years will be noted.

The religious world view of Japan consists of at least five smaller "worlds." These five subworlds can be understood as providing responses to five questions about religious life: what, who, where, when, and how. In other words, these five questions are (1) what are the objects of worship, (2) who are the individuals and social groups involved in these worship activities, (3) where do these rituals of worship take place, (4) when does worship take place, and (5) how are the acts of worship related to human life? This chapter will discuss the Japanese religious world view by focusing on the what of Japanese religion—the objects of worship. The next chapter will discuss the religious world view in terms of who (society), where (space), when (time), and how (human life).[2]

The Sacredness of Kami

First we will look at the what of Japanese religion, the objects of worship. Every religious tradition is oriented around a cluster of objects of worship or principles that define what is "real" or at the heart of life and the universe; by living one's life in harmony with these objects of worship and/or principles, a person experiences a meaningful, rich career and realizes the fulfillment of unity with the essence of the universe. In Japanese religion, at least four major objects of worship (or sources of power) can be singled out: kami, Buddhas, ancestors, and **holy persons**. These four sources of power are closely interrelated both conceptually and in actual practice, just as parts of the human body—the skeleton, muscles, internal organs, and nervous system—are inseparably connected. For the convenience of analysis, the four objects of worship will be treated separately, but frequently the interconnection among them will appear, both in the following four sections and in Chapter IV, which treats other aspects of the world view of Japanese religion. Further illustrations will appear in Chapter V, which gives concrete examples of the dynamics of Japanese religion.

One object of worship and set of principles in Japanese religion is the sacredness of kami, an ancient and persistent feature of the Japanese tradition. Beliefs and practices related to kami have changed considerably, especially in contemporary Japan, but the traditional perception of kami is described here because it is so distinctive of Japanese religion. The notion of kami is very flexible, including whatever within and beyond the world that is extraordinary, in the sense of being sacred and providing the abundance of life. The term *kami* can be either singular or plural and may be translated as "gods," "spirits," or "the sacred" in general. Examples of kami are the mythological deities found in the early writings *Kojiki* and *Nihongi*, emperors as "manifest kami," specific kami of larger shrines, **tutelary kami** (guardian deities) of small local shrines, sacredness as represented by natural phenomena (trees, boulders, waterfalls, mountains), and even living persons (such as founders of New Religions).

The Japanese notion of kami is so different from the doctrine of God in Judaism and Christianity that it is helpful for Westerners to keep in mind the contrast between the two. In the Judeo-Christian tradition, the formal teaching about God emphasizes the transcendent character of the one and only true deity (more than the immanent presence of God within the world and human life). Generally, in both Judaism and Christianity, the relationship between a human being and God involves a formal act of faith, an acknowledgment of the existence of God and a conscious decision to accept God and live in obedience to him. By contrast, kami are many, and although they may hover above the earth, they are also within the forces of nature and within the lives of people. Kami are considered to be everywhere, and traditionally, the Japanese assume the presence of kami as naturally as they see beauty and fertility in nature—no conscious act of faith is needed.

From ancient times, as seen in the *Kojiki* and *Nihongi*, it is recorded that there are myriads of kami, and these kami are woven into the fabric of the life of the Japanese nation and its people. As mentioned briefly in Chapter II, mythological accounts tell of the kami's gradual creation of the Japanese islands, their formation of the imperial line through descent from the Sun Goddess, and their responsibility for the Japanese people. In this fashion, traditionally kami are the force behind both the Japanese landscape and the political entity of the nation and the people. In Japanese religion, people are expected to respond to kami with sincerity and gratitude. Kami also represent the essence of Shinto as the continuation of the beliefs and practices from ancient times. In fact, the term *Shinto* is written with two Chinese characters that can also be pronounced *kami no michi*, "the way of kami." In other words, Shinto is literally the way of life according to kami. In Shinto, kami are characterized not only by sacredness but also by purity, and humans must carefully purify themselves before approaching kami.

Ceremonies for kami can occur in a natural setting, in shrines, or in the home. Pilgrimages to sacred mountains and waterfalls are examples of religious rites in a natural setting. Often a massive boulder or a tall tree will be singled out as a site of prayers by placing a rice straw rope around it. The rice straw rope indicates that the natural object is set apart as special or sacred, in the sense of being the place where kami dwell or can be ritually called down. Simple prayers or more elaborate rituals are performed here. In ancient times probably all religious celebrations were performed in such natural settings, but eventually buildings came to be used as Shinto shrines.

Even within a shrine, there is usually no physical representation of kami (such as a statue). The presence of the kami is assumed, and for special occasions, Shinto priests use formal prayers (norito) to call down kami and convey the blessing of the kami to the assembled people. At the conclusion of the ceremony, priests "send off" the kami. When there is no special occasion, people may approach the

A woman bows her head and joins her hands as she prays before a small shrine of the kami Inari within the grounds of a Buddhist temple in Tokyo. An offering box in front of the woman is where worshipers may drop coins; the small white objects placed against the shrine are porcelain foxes, offered here because Inari is associated with the fox. Inari traditionally was related to agriculture and food, but in cities people generally pray to Inari for good luck and protection.

shrine as individuals. Usually they purify themselves first by rinsing their hands and mouths with water provided inside the shrine grounds; then they walk to the front of a shrine, make a small offering of money, ring a bell, bow their head, and clap their hands several times before saying their prayers silently. Such prayers can be simple requests for safety and blessing, or thanks for previous blessings.

Perhaps the most important ceremonies for kami occur in and around the home. In traditional Japan (especially before the Meiji period, 1868–1911), almost every home was considered affiliated with a local shrine. This local shrine was the sacred site of the local tutelary kami, and people participated in festivals and other ceremonies by virtue of their living within the territory of this local shrine. Families paid visits to the shrine especially at the New Year and for the shrine festivals (such as the spring and fall festivals). Often these local shrines were quite small, too small for many people to enter; such shrines were not intended as congregational gathering places like churches and synagogues. It was customary for parishioners to say their prayers in front of the shrine without entering. Such simple visits to the tutelary kami took place at important times in a person's life.

The home itself is a sacred place partly due to the presence of kami. Traditionally, in the central room of the house there was a special shelf called kamidana (literally, "kami shelf" or "kami altar," sometimes translated as "god shelf"). This shelf or altar usually held a miniature Shinto-style shrine, and offerings of food were presented there morning and evening. Paper amulets or charms from major shrines, such as the Ise Shrine, as well as important regional shrines and the local tutelary deity shrine, were placed on this altar. This was a symbolic means of enshrining the kami of these shrines in the home and requesting their protection and blessing. In Japan the home has been a much more important center of religious activities than it is in contemporary Christian cultures.

The preceding discussion of the sacredness of kami is written in the past tense, describing "traditional" Japan, because these beliefs and practices are not so widespread and faithfully observed today as they once were. From the Meiji period (1868–1911) on, significant changes took place in Japanese society, especially the rapid move from a rural and agricultural life-style to a more urban and industrial-commercial one. As these changes took place, many practices related to kami came to be considered less important or were completely neglected. For example, the movement of families from the countryside to cities and from area to area greatly weakened the traditional pattern of families being affiliated to a local tutelary kami shrine. And with the increasing emphasis on an industrial-commercial society, the agricultural rhythms so important to the honoring of kami have been replaced by the cycle of the work week. In addition, many homes today do not have an altar for kami and do not observe regular ceremonies for kami.

Although traditional observances for kami have declined, they still represent a venerable ideal and are still practiced by many people and actively encouraged by some groups, such as New Religions, thus demonstrating the significance of kami from ancient religion to contemporary times. What are some of the general features of the traditional notions about kami? One of the characteristics of kami that may surprise the Western viewer is the closeness and intimacy of kami. Something extraordinary and awe-inspiring, such as Mount Fuji or a majestic waterfall, or even a nearby hill or stream, can be considered a kami or viewed as expressing the sacredness of kami. And occasionally human beings, such as founders of New Religions, are considered "living kami."

One of the general principles behind these notions is the ideal of close harmony among humans, kami, and nature. The desired human behavior in relationship to kami shows gratitude for the bounty of nature and thanks for the blessing of the kami. In this fashion, there is an intimate and harmonious relationship among the three that benefits all: the purity and sacredness of kami are honored, the rhythm and bounty of nature are preserved, and the sincerity and fullness of human life are enhanced.

Viewed negatively, if humans approach kami in an impure or insincere fashion, the purity of the kami is violated, destroying the harmonious relationship and endangering the protection of kami and the bounty of nature. Living in tune with kami means to maximize this purity and sacredness and to minimize impurity and insincerity. As in any religion, an absolutely pure and sacred state is almost impossible to attain—there is a constant tension between the relatively sacred-pure and the relatively profane-impure. Shinto provides rituals both for regular purification and for special cases of purification. This makes it possible to restore the ideal relationship of harmony among humans, kami, and nature: this sacred harmony is the essence of the world of kami.

The Power of Buddhas

A second object of worship and set of principles in Japanese religion is the power of Buddhas. In some instances the power of Buddhas conflicts with the sacredness of kami, but in most cases the two complement and reinforce each other. In fact the two are so closely interrelated that there is a term in Japanese for "kami and Buddhas" that can be pronounced two ways: the modified Chinese pronunciation is *shin-butsu*, the Japanese style pronunciation is *kami-hotoke*. It is used when referring to both traditions, for example, protection by kami and Buddhas, in other words, "divine" protection. As we have seen in the first and second chapters, Japanese religion combines Shinto and Buddhism, along with other traditions, to construct a total world view. Buddhist scholars and Shinto scholars have had their own theories about the relationship between kami and Buddhist divinities. However, in popular practice, people do not distinguish sharply between help from kami and help from Buddhas.

In Japan, Buddhism became an integral part of Japanese religion, but we must remember that Buddhism is a distinct tradition, possessing its own historical development and specific notions. It may be helpful first to distinguish between the historical Buddha (Gautama) and the many Buddhist divinities loosely called Buddhas. The historical Buddha was a prince named Siddhartha Gautama, who lived in India during the sixth and fifth centuries B.C. and developed the path of enlightenment. He taught that the power of enlightenment was available to all people, in the sense of living life meaningfully, especially overcoming human deficiencies (such as desire and greed) and achieving a peaceful, tranquil state. Thus, Gautama is considered the founder of Buddhism and is called the Buddha, which means "the enlightened one."

After the death of Buddha, his followers organized his teachings into the religion later called Buddhism. This religion came to include many divinities who express, not only the power of enlightenment, but also the power of many practical benefits. These benefits range from being reborn in heavenly paradise to healing of sickness and even the granting of children to women. There are a number of technical terms for such Buddhist divinities granting these benefits, but in general they can all be called Buddhas.

It may seem strange that although the historical Buddha was the founder of Buddhism, in Japan there are fewer statues and less direct worship of this Buddha than there are statues and direct worship of the many Buddhist divinities, or Buddhas. One reason for this apparent contradiction is that the various divisions of Buddhist sects and denominations developed around specific teachings and particular Buddhist divinities. Another reason is that rather few people follow the difficult path of the historical Buddha to the power of enlightenment; many more seek out the specific powers of practical benefits granted by Buddhist divinities.

The elaborate statues of Buddhas within Buddhist temples create a different atmosphere from that of the rather "empty" space of Shinto shrines. Within Shinto shrines there are usually no statues, and one has to sense the presence of the kami just as one has to appreciate the beauty of nature even when it is not identified with a sign. There is a naturalness and freshness to a Shinto shrine that is hard to describe; it is expressed in the restraint of the decoration, and it creates an air of quiet peace. By contrast, the elaborate altar and statues of Buddhist temples can seem overwhelming. To sit in a dark temple with the flicker of candles casting light and shadow on gilded Buddhist statues is a memorable experience.

Ceremonies for Buddhas take place in large headquarters of Buddhist sects, in regional temples, in local parish temples, in small chapels, and in the home. Buddhism is more highly institutionalized than Shinto, and there is more ecclesiastical structure in Buddhism—for example, the tie between a headquarters temple and its branch temples. The larger temples tend to combine some bureaucratic management with facilities for the study and practice of Buddhism. But most temples, large or small, enshrine Buddhist statues before which scriptures are recited and rituals performed. All these activities indirectly or directly are attempts to gain enlightenment and to request the help of Buddhas.

There are many Buddhas, and each has its own special benefits. **Kannon**, the goddess of mercy, is one of the most popular Buddhas, partly because Kannon grants requests for almost any kind of help. One specific form of Kannon, called Koyasu Kannon, or "Easy Childbirth Kannon," is popular with married women who want to conceive a child or who seek help in giving birth. Another form of Kannon, Bato Kannon ("Horseheaded Kannon"), once was popular with people who used horses and cows as beasts of burden, but even in highly mechanized contemporary Japan, Bato Kannon still has some followers.

Jizo is the patron saint of spirits of the dead, especially of dead children. Statues of Jizo, like other Buddhas, are found not only in large temples but also in wayside chapels (too small to enter), and such statues are seen even in the open air. Particularly for Jizo, a popular practice is to stack piles of stones near the statue (thought to help the spirits of dead children accumulate merit), and often candies and crackers are offered to Jizo.

Yakushi is the healing Buddha, and people who are sick or who are praying for a sick person will pay a visit to a Yakushi statue. The usual act of devotion before a Buddhist statue is to recite a brief passage from a Buddhist scripture; this helps enlighten the person

A child uses a dipper to splash water on a statue of Jizo, a Buddhist divinity. This statue is next to a cemetery; during the festival of the dead in late summer families visit cemeteries to make offerings and burn incense at family memorial stones (note the smoke above the head of the small girl). Pouring water over memorial stones or splashing water on a Buddhist statue is a means of purifying the spirits of the dead or honoring a Buddhist divinity.

and incorporates within the person the power of the scripture and the statue.

Amida rivals Kannon and Jizo as one of the most important Buddhas. There are many physical representations of Amida that attract followers, but Amida is prayed to directly (even when no statue is present) by reciting the phrase *namu Amida Butsu* ("I place my faith in Amida Buddha"). Amida grants believers who practice this recitation assurance of rebirth in Amida's paradise after death. On medieval battlefields this cry was uttered by the wounded and dying who sought comfort from Amida, and it is still popular today.

These are but a few of the countless Buddhas honored within Japanese Buddhism. One interesting aspect of the veneration of these Buddhas is that most activities are carried out by laypersons with little or no priestly help and no national structure linking either the sites of worship for a Buddha or the followers of a Buddha. Often a group of laypeople in a local area form their own association or club for the worship of a particular Buddha, such as Kannon, and hold monthly meetings in homes, combining a social gathering with a simple service honoring Kannon. If members of such an association collect enough money, they might buy a small stone statue of Kannon and have it erected nearby. This is a good example of the presence of Buddhas in the life of the people.

Another aspect of the power of Buddhas is that the founders of Buddhist sects may also be considered as extremely powerful and able to grant benefits to believers. Nichiren, the founder of the Nichiren sect, declared himself to be the reincarnation of a previous Buddha. And Kobo Daishi is very popular in folktales—for example, one tale tells that because a kind girl walked a long distance to bring Kobo Daishi a drink of water, he used his staff to make a spring of water come forth so that she would not have to go so far for water. Such founders possess the power of Buddhas and are similar to "living kami."

People may travel to the headquarters of the parish Buddhist temple to which their family belongs or visit a regional temple that is famous for certain statues or for certain powers. Usually when a person enters such larger temples, a small amount of money is donated; also, incense is bought and lit from an altar candle and placed upright in a container filled with sand. Incense is a common offering to both Buddhas and spirits of the dead. A person may visit the family parish temple for special occasions, but the crucial link between the family and this temple is the family ancestors. Probably the most significant power of Buddhism, from a popular standpoint, is the use of Buddhist rituals to help transform the corpses of family dead into purified ancestors who grant blessings to the family. We will see in the next section that ancestors are one of the central features of Japanese religion. Funerals and memorials for family dead are conducted by Buddhist priests and temples, and this is the main source of income for such parish temples. In Tokugawa times (1600–1867), the government required each family to belong to a Buddhist temple, and even though this requirement was dropped after the opening of the Meiji era in 1868, most families have retained affiliation to a parish Buddhist temple.

In most homes it has been the custom to have a Buddhist altar (butsudan) in the main room of the house. Many traditional homes have had both Buddhist altar and Shinto altar (kamidana) in the same central room (one exception is families belonging to Pure Land denominations, which prohibit the use of kamidana). The Buddhist altar, an expensive lacquered or finished cabinet, contains, not only pictures and statues of Buddhas, and small containers for offerings of food, but more important, the wooden tablets representing the spirits of the family ancestors. It is interesting that a common word for ancestor, *hotoke*, can also mean "Buddha." Thus, an ancestor is considered a Buddha or has the power of a Buddha. Pious Japanese make daily offerings to the "Buddhas" (Buddhist divinities and family ancestors) and recite short sections of Buddhist scriptures in front of the Buddhist altar. In modern Japan more homes have Buddhist altars than Shinto altars, probably because of the greater strength of the family bond (which is expressed through the Buddhist altar as respect for family ancestors).

The power of the Buddha and specific Buddhas is quite diverse, ranging from the lofty notion of enlightenment to very practical benefits. These two ideals—enlightenment and practical benefits— may seem contradictory, but actually they are only different aspects of the same principle. This principle is to live as close to the ideals of Buddhism as possible, eliminating personal defects and powerlessness and maximizing personal power. The way to a more powerful life may come either by following the example of the historical Buddha, overcoming uncontrolled emotions in order to become enlightened and living a life of tranquility and compassion for others, or by relying directly on the help of various Buddhist divinities to gain specific powers for solving problems in this life. (In the case of Amida, power is sought to assure peace in the next life.) In ancient times the powerful resources of Buddhas were monopolized by the state, but later, especially from Tokugawa times on, the power of Buddhas became an integral part of village and home life. Buddhist statues on village streets and Buddhist altars in homes brought the people in close daily contact with the presence and power of Buddhas. The world of Buddhas is both the power of enlightenment and the power to live.

The Blessings of Ancestors

A third object of worship and set of principles in Japanese religion is the blessings of ancestors. The role of ancestors is central to Japanese religion, but to understand this role, we must recognize the difference between the rather casual notion of ancestors in the West and the more significant concept of ancestors in Japan. In European and American usage, ancestors are all the dead people from whom a person is descended, both on the father's and the mother's side. Ancestry is considered part of a person's biological and social past, but it is of little importance for living one's life and is of no consequence religiously.

By contrast, in Japan ancestors refer especially to those from whom a person is descended in the father's line, as a continuation of family succession that directly affects personal fortune and religious behavior. Ancestors are much more than a biological and social fact, because family members do not automatically become ancestors when they die. Both a lapse of time and the transforming power of ritual are necessary to change the impure corpse into a purified ancestor. Religion is directly involved in the creation of ancestors: the major result of this ritual transformation is that the impure dead person becomes a benevolent source of blessings for descendants. Not only is a funeral performed for family dead, but memorial rites continue for many years, and a family prays to ancestors for protection and blessing.

Some features of ancestors have been seen in the earlier discussion of the power of Buddhas: ancestors are enshrined in the home in Buddhist altars called butsudan, before which simple offerings and recitations are made by family members. But exactly how does a person become an ancestor? The major procedures for handling the dead are Buddhist, especially since the time of the dominance of Buddhism during the Tokugawa period (1600–1867). In almost every culture, dead bodies and death generally are considered impure or defiling, and Japan is no exception. Ancient Japanese custom for disposing of the impure corpse was burial, but the Buddhist practice of cremation gradually became accepted and is standard today (encouraged partly for health reasons). The symbolism of cremation itself is clearly a means of driving out the impurity by destroying it with fire; in the smoke of cremation the "spirit" of the dead person ascends. Ashes of the person remaining after cremation are put in a small container and placed in the parish Buddhist temple to which the family belongs.

The key Buddhist ritual is the funeral mass, and subsequent memorial masses. Details of such rituals vary considerably from denomination to denomination, but the gist of all these rituals is to transform the impure corpse into a purified being, or ancestor. During the funeral mass, Buddhist scriptures are recited by priests to draw on their power as a means of transforming the dead person. As part of the transformation process, the Buddhist priest grants the dead person a special posthumous name, or "Buddhist name." This honorary name indicates, in Buddhist terms, that the material aspect of the dead person has been extinguished, and the person has gone on to enlightenment, or paradise. The Buddhist name is written on a memorial tablet for the individual; memorial tablets are used in the home for subsequent memorial rites. The time that it takes a dead person to be elevated to enlightenment or paradise varies with different denominations, but usually there are forty-nine days of mourning after death. This is considered the end of a period of impurity for both the dead person and his or her family. In formal Buddhist teaching, this indicates that the dead person has completed passage through stages of hell and is reborn; in popular understanding this means that the dead person's impurity has been eliminated and the person has been transformed into a benevolent ancestor.

To illustrate the significance of ancestors, it may help to explain the opposite situation—when a dead person does not become an ancestor. If the proper funeral and memorial rites are not performed for a dead person, there is always the possibility that the dead spirit will wander around the world and haunt people, causing misfortune and sickness not only for the dead person's family but for nearby people as well. There are special rituals to specify such dead persons with "no relatives" so that they do not cause problems. This is a good example of the Japanese tendency to view human identity as an interrelationship of people, rather than as an individual existence. Both in life and in death, to be merely an individual (with no relation to other persons) is a dangerous condition, almost the same as being no one, having no identity. The dead individual who is not regularly memorialized is not transformed from impure corpse to pure ancestor, and therefore the person suffers and may also cause the living to suffer.

After memorial tablets are placed in the Buddhist altar in the home, they are regularly honored by the family with simple offerings and brief passages of scripture. The Buddhist priest of the family's parish temple is requested to perform memorial masses, especially on the annual anniversary of the person's death, and may come to the home for this purpose. Ritual observance of this "death day" is practiced for many years—usually thirty-three or fifty—after which the individual memorial tablet is no longer honored in the butsudan. According to Japanese custom, ancestors make special visits to family homes during the New Year celebrations and during the festival of the dead in late summer—these are two of the most important annual festivals.

The religious significance of the home is clear from the presence of ancestors in the home and the regular performance of rituals by the family in relationship to ancestors. In fact, the butsudan, whose literal translation is "Buddhist altar" might just as well be called a "family altar" or "ancestral altar," since the ancestral tablets are valued more highly than the Buddhist statues and pictures in the altar. If a house catches fire, the first thing to be saved is this altar, and if there is not time to save the entire altar, memorial tablets will be saved and Buddhist statues will be left behind.[3] This is perhaps an extreme example, but it shows that the blessing of ancestors is crucial to the values of the Japanese family.

Other aspects of ancestors highlight the significance of this family altar. Traditionally, ancestors were considered primarily through the father, and the first son of a family continued the family line, which meant keeping the ancestral tablets of the family. In some instances this continuation of the family line by the first son was called the main family, and other sons set up branch families. In traditional settings, it was customary for branch families to pay respects at the home of the main family, especially at the New Year, partly out of deference to their common ancestors. In the traditional setting, only the main family had a large butsudan; a branch family would buy a rather modest butsudan only when a member of this branch family died. In recent times customs have become much more flexible: there is less emphasis on main and branch families, and usually a family buys a butsudan after the first death in the immediate family.

The blessing that ancestors provide is life itself and protection within the ongoing unit of the family. Life is precious, and each person owes a debt to parents and ancestors for this gift of life. Members of a family pray to ancestors for offspring, health, and prosperity. In Japan, as in other countries, the family is the basic social unit for nurturing life and sharing experience. One of the distinctive features of the Japanese family, at least in contrast to the American family, is that the Japanese family extends from the dead ancestors through the living to the unborn in the future. The family is a religious institution in its own right, with family ancestors as its own objects of worship and the head of the family as its own leader of worship. The world of ancestors is defined by the mutual interaction of descendants providing sincere worship to ancestors and ancestors granting life and blessings to descendants.

Mediation by Holy Persons

A fourth object of worship and set of principles in Japanese religion is the mediation of sacredness and power by holy persons. There are holy persons or saints in most religions, but these figures have special significance in Japanese religion because they are not just holy in the sense of being more devout and set apart from others: in Japan holy persons mediate religious power and may become objects of worship themselves. Our treatment of kami, Buddhas, and ancestors has demonstrated that "deities" in Japanese religion are not far removed from human life; also, humans easily cross the boundary into sacredness and power. *Holy person* is a general term to indicate the kind of person who in his or her lifetime (and/or after death) is an object of worship or mediator of power for many people. Three major representatives of holy persons are (1) the founders of major Buddhist movements, some of whom are considered sources of Buddhist power; (2) the founders of New Religions during the past hundred and fifty years, some of whom are considered living kami; and (3) **shamans** within folk religion, who are mediums between this world and the next, between living and dead. We will look at the three kinds of holy persons separately, starting with founders.

Founders are important in any society or religion, because not only do they initiate an idea and incorporate the idea in a social group but they also as founders represent models to be followed. In Japanese society, founders of movements (even artistic movements) are accorded special attention. Founders of Buddhist movements are singled out here because they are good examples of holy persons from earlier times who are still very important today. The power of Buddhist founders comes partly from the fact that they located the power of Buddhism for other people, making it available for a wider audience. In Japan this usually means that ordinary followers seek the power of Buddhism by believing in a founder, and practice devotions to a founder in order to obtain this power. The Buddhist founder is a model and also a means of obtaining power.

Two cases already mentioned of Buddhist founders as sources of power are Nichiren and Kobo Daishi. Nichiren was a very forceful personality who insisted on the absolute truth of the Lotus Sutra and absolute faith in this Buddhist scripture both for personal salvation and for national welfare. In fact he felt that he was the reincarnation of an earlier Buddha for the purpose of spreading this message. In other words, Nichiren told his followers that he had been born in the form of a Buddhist divinity. This made him an absolute authority on the absolute truth; it is not surprising that followers have worshiped Nichiren down to the present day. Some believers even worship the title of the Lotus Sutra in Nichiren's handwriting, preserved in a major Nichiren temple.

Kobo Daishi was mentioned previously as the founder of the sect of esoteric Buddhism and a popular figure in folk legends. This founder is also worshiped, and there are many informal associations or clubs for this specific purpose. In the name Kobo Daishi, *daishi* is an honorary title that is literally "great teacher" or "saint." A number of Buddhist leaders were granted the title daishi, but the term *daishi*-ko, or "great teacher association," usually means a group of people who gather monthly for the purpose of worshiping Kobo Daishi. He is popularly believed to have been the one who devised the Japanese form of writing, so the power that he represents is both cultural and religious.

One scholar has called this tendency to focus on the power of individuals "the attitude of absolute devotion to a specific individual."[4] This scholar quotes the devotion of Shinran (1173–1262) to his teacher Honen, the founder of Pure Land Buddhism, which centers around recitation of the **nembutsu** (faith in Amida). Shinran wrote: "I do not know whether the nembutsu is actually the means to rebirth in the Pure Land, or whether perhaps it is the road to Hell. Even though I were cajoled by Saint Honen that I should go to Hell through the nembutsu, I should do so and not regret it." This shows the importance in Japanese religion of faith in an individual, rather than in the doctrine taught by the individual. This kind of "absolute devotion" is not limited to founders of Buddhist movements, but they are representative examples.

More recent examples of holy persons are the founders of New

Religions during the past century and a half. Many of these have been women of extraordinary personal and religious experience who both founded New Religions and became objects of worship in their own New Religions. One is Mrs. Miki Nakayama (1798–1887), the founder of the New Religion called Tenrikyo. She became possessed by a deity while helping in a healing ritual for her son. Such temporary possessions were not unusual. What was remarkable is that this deity refused to leave her body, insisting that Mrs. Nakayama should spread the message of rejecting materialism and selfishness for a true religious life. This founder is an example of *ikigami*, a "living kami," a human being who at the same time is filled with kami or is a kami.

For a person to be a kami can mean that everything associated with the person is also kami or sacred, and this has been true for Mrs. Nakayama. Her life and deeds became the sacred models for the religion she founded. Her writings became scriptures. Her songs became hymns. Her gestures became liturgy. To this day she is followed in the teaching and actual liturgy of Tenrikyo, as well as being worshiped herself. Another interesting aspect of Tenrikyo, shared with some other New Religions (and some Buddhist sects), is that the sacred character of the founding figure is inherited by descendants. After the death of Mrs. Nakayama, Tenrikyo has been headed by a line of male descendants; each successor has the title *shinbashira*, usually translated as "patriarch," but the literal meaning is "sacred (kami) pillar." Even when it is a woman who founds a New Religion, the hereditary transmission is usually to male descendants.

This is only one of many interesting examples of holy persons, especially living kami, in New Religions. Mrs. Nakayama's career is but one instance in a rich and varied tradition of founders of New Religions. Many were female, but there have also been male founders. Some gained their kami character through possessions, like Mrs. Nakayama; others received a revelation from a deity, yet others underwent strict religious training as a means of acquiring power. Whatever the founder's approach to sacredness and power, followers usually have considered these founders as worthy of worship and as channels for obtaining power and blessings.

Holy persons are not limited to the founders of large movements. Another important category of holy person in Japanese religion is the "shaman" or medium who lives among people and serves individuals apart from organized movements. There are many local variations of such mediums, each given a particular Japanese name. The word *shaman* is a term used by ethnologists to refer to individuals with special religious powers, such as the ability to go into a trance and become a medium between this world and other worlds.

One important tradition of shamans in northern Japan is the blind female who undergoes special training and is able to talk with the dead. Such a shaman lives in an ordinary home (sometimes with other family members) and attracts people through word of mouth by those who have made use of her services. Usually people come to this shaman for specific requests to speak to a dead relative, such as asking what offerings should be made for that person. A fee is paid, and the request is given to the shaman, who performs a ritual in order to get into contact with the dead spirit. The shaman makes offerings before a simple altar in the home and recites a simple liturgy she has learned as part of her training. The climax of the service is when she enters a trancelike state, at which time she becomes the mouthpiece for the dead relative and will answer simple questions put to her. After a brief exchange with the dead relative, the trancelike state ends and the person requesting the ritual leaves.

In this tradition of blind female shamans, there is a rather rigorous training period. The young woman may experience a "call" by a certain deity, indicating that she should become a shaman. She must find a senior shaman who will accept her for training and then undergo years of practice. She learns the rituals, recitations, and techniques of entering trance and speaking with the dead. Usually there is an intense initiation symbolizing marriage to the deity who called her. This initiation qualifies her to become a shaman and set up her own altar for communicating with the dead.

This brief description of the blind female shaman is but one example of the shamans within Japanese religion and does not include other kinds of holy persons who are able to draw on power and sacredness. This example was selected because it is a good illustration of a holy person as a mediator of power (rather than an object of worship). People who have specific problems and particular requests of the dead want to communicate with the other world, but ordinary people cannot do this. Only a person who has undergone special training and gained special power can become a medium between this world and the next, and traditionally the Japanese have perceived the blind female shaman to be able to do this. Today this kind of shaman is becoming rare, but there are a number of other kinds of holy persons who have similar powers.

The general principle that applies to holy persons in Japanese religion is that sacredness and power are not completely outside the world but are often found within the world in living human beings (or human beings who once were alive). Some individuals, such as Nichiren, seem to have talent and persistence in pursuing religious power. Some people seem to become kami partly by accident, as in Mrs. Nakayama's accidental possession. Other founders of New Religions may undergo strict religious practice, and shamans may have to train for years before they are initiated. However this power is acquired, the understanding is that ordinary people, who do not have such powers, may make use of such power by following the model of holy persons: by imitating their practices (such as reciting the nembutsu), by worshiping the holy person, and/or by making requests to the holy person (through prayers or through direct request to a shaman).

The kami, Buddhas, ancestors, and holy persons interrelate to form a cluster of objects of worship and principles around which Japanese religion is organized. As a group of interrelated sources of sacredness, power, blessing, and mediation, they enable one to define what is "real," or at the heart of life and the universe. By conforming one's own life to this ideal picture of what is real and meaningful, one can experience a rich and rewarding career. Inevitably, as with any living system, there are tensions among these four objects of worship. However, most of the time they interact with each other in harmonious fashion to shape and support the Japanese religious world view.

A person does not rely on just one object of worship but depends on all of them to lead a full religious life. Kami provide for the sacredness of local areas as local tutelary deities. Buddhas provide power as a philosophy of life and as solutions to particular problems. Ancestors nourish and sustain family life with blessings and protection. Holy persons mediate the richness of these traditions for ordinary people, making it possible for them to participate more fully in these sources of sacredness and power. The "world" of holy persons is a point of contact between powerless people and powerful founders, a bridge between this life and the next life.

These objects of worship are not separate from one another but constantly interact and overlap. Just as the Shinto altar (kamidana) and Buddhist altar (butsudan) are found in the same room, and just as Buddhas and ancestors are enshrined in the same Buddhist altar, these objects are organic parts of a living system. As a whole, these objects of worship define the what of the universe of Japanese religion. However, there is more to the universe of religion than the objects of worship. In the next chapter we will examine other aspects of the world view of Japanese religion, looking more closely at four smaller worlds of religious life: who (society), where (space), when (time), and how (life).

CHAPTER IV

Japanese Religion's World View

O bjects of worship provide the what around which the world view of Japanese religion is centered. Four smaller worlds revolve around this center of worship: the organization of religious life in terms of who worships (society), where worship takes place (space), when worship takes place (time), and how worship directly affects people (human life). Each of these smaller religious worlds will be treated separately.

The Religious World of Society

The world view of Japanese religion has been examined in terms of the objects of worship (such as kami and Buddhas); it can also be seen in terms of the subjects of worship (the people who carry out the worship). The present section focuses on the who of religion, the human rather than the divine. The way in which individuals and groups are involved in religion is an important factor in the practice of religious life. The religious world of society is the formation and use of social units (individuals and groups) for the purpose of preserving, celebrating, and transmitting religion. The role of individuals and groups varies from culture to culture. For example, in a modern country like the United States, the human organization of religion is usually considered as the relationship between an individual and a specially formed religious group such as a church or synagogue. In modern Japan, there is a similar pattern of relationship between an individual and a special religious group (for example, in a New Religion). But on the whole, Japanese religion presents a striking contrast with religion in modern America. During the past few centuries of Japanese religion, the individual has played less of a role than the family; also, special religious groups (such as churches) have been less important than ordinary social groups such as family, village, and nation. In fact, these "social" groups derive part of their identity and character from their involvement in religion. The major role of these social groups becomes apparent as we discuss units of human organization of religion in Japan: individual, family, village, nation, and specific religious groups.

The individual is less important in Japanese religion than in modern Western religion. In Japan people have participated in religion more as members of groups than as individuals; especially from Tokugawa times on, the family and village have been the major means of participating in religion. Not to be a member of such a group practically eliminates a person from participating in religion. A good example has already been seen in the ritual transformation of ancestors. One becomes an ancestor not through one's own achievements, virtue, or "salvation," but through the rituals that other family members perform (and have priests perform). If the funeral and memorial rites are not properly performed, then one is not transformed into a benevolent ancestor and is doomed to wander the earth and haunt people. The ideal, of course, is to have descendants perform the proper funeral and memorial rites so that the dead person can benefit the family line with protection and blessing. In death as in life, religious fulfillment is channeled more through groups than through individual existence.

Emphasis on group participation in religion does not mean that there is no individual experience in religion; rather, it means that religion is organized and experienced in the context of groups. This can be demonstrated in the Zen Buddhist ideal of being enlightened through meditation—which has often been misunderstood outside Japan as a highly individualistic experience. Enlightenment (or "awakening") does occur to individuals, but usually to individuals who are in the context of a Zen monastery—which is a tightly controlled community with rigid scheduling not only of meditation but of every detail of life from waking to sleeping. An individual who reaches the point of experiencing enlightenment does so by virtue of relationship to a Zen master and by means of the heightened concentration achieved within the structure of the monastic community. The family may be considered the cornerstone of Japanese society as well as of Japanese religion. A Japanese person has a very strong sense of identity as a member of a family, much stronger than his or her identity as an individual. Ideally a person should always think and act with family interest ahead of personal interest. Participation in religion usually has been as a family, rather than by individual decision. Family residence determines participation in the Shinto shrine of the local tutelary kami; family birth determines participation in the hereditary Buddhist parish. These are the two most important centers of religious activity outside the home, and both are entered as a family rather than as an individual.

As we have seen, the family is a religious institution in its own right, with ancestors constituting the objects of worship, the male head acting as leader in worship, and the family as a unit serving as members of the religious institution. The particular anniversaries of death days observed by each family mean that a family even has its own calendar of religious events. The family home is the site of one or more altars. The family is practically a miniature religion itself, as is demonstrated in the family's inclusion of its own objects of worship (ancestors in the butsudan). As one scholar has phrased it, "Certain types of psychological security found in a relationship to a personal God in the West are found only in relation to the actual family in Japan."[5]

Social relationships are so important that ethical relationships are expressed more through social relationships than through universal principles; the family situation is the best example. The strong influence of Confucian thinking, developed especially during Tokugawa society, has shaped Japanese attitudes of filial piety and loyalty. Filial piety is the reverential obedience of children to parents: because parents give life to children, children can never repay the debt they owe parents. Children should defer completely to parents (even when the "children" themselves are adults). Obedience to parents and reverence for ancestors are two of the basic virtues in Japanese society and religion. Parents are benevolent and protective of children. This model of social harmony in the family is the pattern for loyalty and benevolence outside the family in the local community, in work relationships, and in the nation as a whole.

Families participate in a local community, which for traditional

Japan has been the village, and for modern urban Japan is more frequently a city or a district of a city. The traditional village pattern, although mostly replaced with city patterns, is important because it helped shape an understanding of life that is still influential today.

In the traditional countryside a number of farming families formed a small village community (or a smaller unit). The traditional village was the basic unit of economic and religious cooperation. In farming villages rice was a main crop for taxes and cash, and growing rice in irrigated fields required considerable cooperation. It was necessary for all the farmers in an area around a water source to agree on the time of planting and even the hours when water flowed from one field to another. Such practical decisions and many other matters affecting the common good of the community were decided in village councils. The village also cooperated to hold village celebrations. Such festivities varied greatly from village to village but usually included annual festivals such as the New Year and other seasonal rituals as well as special local traditions. The New Year is a ritual opening of the year and an asking of blessings for the villagers. In some areas there were elaborate rituals accompanying rice transplanting and festivals after the rice harvest; this defines a widespread spring and fall cycle of ritual in Japanese religion.

Most of these village celebrations were carried out by the villagers themselves, often without any professional religious leaders. Male heads of leading families often took turns being in charge of the rituals, and other leading families played key roles. In many villages it was the custom that a family had to live there for several generations before the male head of the family could participate in community decision-making councils and help perform annual festivals. Each village had its own customs and traditions about what celebrations would be held, when, and who could participate. Often young men were allowed to play a role in some public part of a festival, such as carrying a large wooden altar through the streets, as part of the recognition of their passing into manhood.

It is difficult to describe a general pattern for village religion, since there is so much local variation. But a universal feature is that one did not consciously "decide" to participate in a village festival—one did so almost automatically, by virtue of membership in the village and according to one's status in the village. Religion did not create such villages, but it did help define the village as a religious community by mobilizing it for the performance of rituals by and for the local community. Even in cities, an area of a city performed annual rituals (especially the New Year, spring, and fall festivals) in a fashion similar to the village pattern. In modern Japan, especially after World War II, village festivals have been neglected, partly because of the rapid shift of the population from the countryside to the city. The weakening of involvement in traditional local celebrations is one factor that has encouraged participation in special religious groups like New Religions.

The nation is the largest social unit related to Japanese religion. Like the family and the village, the nation is considered primarily a social and political unit, but it has had a specific religious character in the past and continues to have a semireligious character today. As we have seen in previous chapters, traditional mythology describes the nation as a country founded by kami, led by an emperor who is descended from kami, and inhabited by a people united in worship of these kami and in loyalty to the emperor. In other words, from ancient times, "Japanese people" meant more than inhabitants of a certain area; it meant a group of people united by common practices of religious life.

One representative feature of this "national" religion is the Ise Shrine, where the Sun Goddess (from whom the imperial line is descended) is enshrined. This is considered the holiest of Shinto shrines, and since medieval times it has been popular practice to make pilgrimages there. Pilgrims take back special blessings to their homes, and many families buy a paper form of blessing from Ise annually to place in their kamidana (Shinto-style altar).

Another feature of the "national" religion is the round of rituals performed by the emperor for the sake of the Japanese people. Especially at harvest time, the emperor holds a special thanksgiving rite, and the enthronement ceremony for a new emperor is patterned after this rite. In traditional times the people had little contact with the emperor, but he carried out these religious activities behind the scenes; since World War II this has raised legal questions. It is well to remember that through the centuries there were various political forms, and the emperor never ruled Japan directly. In fact, the strong sense of patriotic and national identity as a country founded by kami and guided by the emperor is a more recent development from the Meiji era (1868–1911) down through World War II. The close association of religious support for nationalism, colonialism, and militarism leading up to World War II has caused widespread concern in Japan. Legally, the constitution written after World War II protects freedom of religion; it prohibits government support of any religion as well as discrimination against any religion. However, what the constitution means in actual practice is something still being debated today. One of the constitutional questions is whether national funds can and should be used to support the Ise Shrine and the rituals performed by the emperor. The relationship between religious commitment and national identity is a problem for Japan, just as it is for many other modern nations. In contemporary Japan the rather literal interpretation of the emperor as descended from kami and leading the Japanese people in the worship of kami is not widely held. But some scholars feel that, indirectly, much motivation for the enthusiasm, efficiency, and cooperation of the Japanese people in achieving economic success is a modern expression of the earlier notion of a "sacred" national entity.

Social units such as family, village, and nation have played major roles in Japanese religion, and special religious groups—those formed specifically for religious purposes—have been less important. There are institutional aspects of Japanese religion, especially Buddhism, however, that resemble some aspects of denominationalism in Protestant Christianity: there are numerous denominations of Buddhist sects, for example, subdivisions of Tendai and Shingon. But a family thinks of its affiliation to a local temple more as a parish Buddhist temple that helps memorialize family ancestors than as belonging to a particular Buddhist denomination. The consciousness of denominational ties is so weak that many people do not even know the exact denominational affiliation of their local parish temple.

One of the strongest traditional forms of the special religious group is the association or club (ko) formed locally for the purpose of honoring a particular deity, usually a Buddha such as Kannon. Sometimes a whole village belonged to this association; sometimes individuals joined freely. This informal group met at regular intervals (usually monthly) in homes to worship Kannon or another Buddha without any priestly supervision, and several members of the association used modest association funds to make a pilgrimage to a regional center honoring their object of worship. Such associations, because of their strong grassroots character, formed one of the most important special religious groups in traditional Japan. Some of these associations are still active today, but they have tended to decline along with other traditional village practices.

Since the nineteenth century, and especially in the twentieth century, New Religions have become the most important special religious groups. To become a member of a New Religion, it is necessary (at least for the first generation of members) to make a decision to join. In contrast to the traditional patterns of religious affiliation—the residential tie to the Shinto shrine of the local tutelary kami and the hereditary tie to the local parish Buddhist temple—a person has to make a conscious step to join a New Religion. The relationship between an individual and a New Religion is the closest parallel to the Western pattern of an individual joining a church. However, there are also some striking differences, since a member of a Christian church in a Western country usually does not form any other religious ties, whereas a Japanese member of a New Religion may continue to participate in several other religious groups.

Individuals join a New Religion when they are convinced of the truth of the teaching or the effectiveness of the ritual, often through the introduction of a relative or neighbor. Frequently an individual faces a personal problem, such as sickness or family tension, that prompts the quest for a religious answer. When the person is convinced of the New Religion's power to resolve this problem and meet the religious need, he or she joins the New Religion. Membership is in both a local branch and the nationwide religion, unifying all Japanese (and often foreign) members in the same forms of worship and principles of life. These nationwide and universal units of religious membership have increased in number and strength as village and local forms of religion have declined. But New Religions do not necessarily contradict or oppose traditional religious life; in fact, they often incorporate and renew traditional forms. The relation between the founder of a New Religion and an individual member is often seen as a "parent-child" relationship—the "child" (individual) should be grateful, obedient, and reverent to the "parent" (founder) who provides protection and blessing. In this fashion, traditional Confucian and family values are re-created in the framework of a New Religion.

The who of religious organization in Japan traditionally emphasized ordinary social units such as family and village, with some special religious groups, like the informal associations (ko), and also the nation as a whole. In modern Japan, especially after World War II, New Religions are the most conspicuous and successful means of organizing people for religious purposes.

The Religious World of Space

Previous sections have approached the world view of Japanese religion through what is worshiped (objects of worship) and who does the worshiping (social groups); next we examine where the worship takes place, or the religious world of space. In the West, religious space is closely associated with churches and synagogues, since they are dedicated to the worship of God. In Japan there are similar examples of sacred space associated with deities enshrined in religious buildings (such as Shinto shrines and Buddhist temples), but in Japan sacred space is not so strictly limited to specific religious buildings. Space is considered as sacred wherever objects of worship are enshrined or wherever people can come into contact with them. Major locations of sacred space in Japanese religion are the home, village or local sacred sites, regional or special sacred sites, and national sacred sites. All these locations represent sacred space set aside for humans to contact objects of worship. Some of these places of sacred space correspond roughly to the units of society treated in the preceding section. For example, the family was discussed as the basic social and religious unit; correspondingly, the home is a basic location of sacred space. We are now looking at the home as space, rather than the family as social unit.

The traditional home was sacred in the sense that it was built with the aid of religious rituals and continually honored with various rituals. There was a special ritual to consecrate the building site before the house was started, as well as a special ritual for completion of the house frame, signified by the raising of the ridgepole. Various parts of the traditional house were considered sacred—the threshold, the central pillar, the kitchen, and even the toilet. Kami resided in these places, and some larger houses had a special family shrine on the land surrounding the house. Many of these traditional practices have fallen into disuse, but even some New Religions continue practices that honor the sacred character of the home.

The home is sacred also due to the presence of altars (and objects of worship) in the home. It has been common for many homes to have both a kamidana (Shinto-style altar) and a butsudan (Buddhist-style altar). The kamidana helps make the home sacred by enshrining kami in the home; these may be the local tutelary kami, or the kami of more distant shrines, even the Ise Shrine. One means of enshrining kami is by making a visit to a shrine and paying a small fee for a special shrine paper with the seal of the shrine and its protective blessing; the paper is placed in the home (sometimes in the kamidana), but is usually removed and burned at the New Year, when it is replaced with another. The butsudan is doubly sa-

A kamidana (Shinto-style altar) displayed for sale in a Tokyo department store: the price of 69,900 yen is equivalent to about $300. When purchased, this type of small Shinto shrine is placed on a high shelf in the main room of a home, and kami are enshrined (often by means of papers bought at Shinto shrines and placed in the kamidana); small offering vessels will be placed on or before the kamidana to make offerings of food.

A rather ornate butsudan (Buddhist-style altar) in the home of a man who also serves
as a leader of Buddhist services in a rural area. Because this altar also is used for
Buddhist worship services, the central figure is a statue of Amida, one of the most
important Buddhist divinities. Memorial tables are often placed within the altar,
but this family has a separate table for ancestral tablets to the left of the altar (not
visible in the picture). The memorial tablet at the left (with four Chinese characters
arranged vertically) is a general tablet for spirits of the war dead. A metal vessel for
offering incense is in front of the statue; flowers and fruit are offered at the side of the
altar. The gilded lotus flowers are an important part of Buddhism, because the lotus
grows in mud, but rises out of the mud to bloom as a pure white flower; similarly,
humans can rise above the mud and filth of the world to bloom as enlightened beings.
(Photo courtesy of Dr. Robert J. Smith, Department of Anthropology, Cornell
University.)

cred because it enshrines Buddhas and ancestors, both of which are
objects of worship and sources of blessing. Not only are offerings

and rituals performed before the butsudan, but also special events in the life of the family are "announced" to the ancestors in front of the butsudan.

Traditionally, a number of other aspects of the home have made it sacred, including the seasonal events that center partly around the home. At the New Year, special decorations of evergreens are hung on the house gate; today these are just decorations, but they former-ly signified the renewal of life. Twice a year, at the New Year and at the midsummer festival of the dead, spirits of family ancestors make a special visit to the home, and all family members should try to be present at this time, which is a happy occasion of homecoming for both the living and the dead.

Thus, the home is built with the aid of rituals, enshrines objects of worship, and is the site of frequent festivities. More than modern Western homes, the Japanese home defines an important sacred space; it enables the family to come into contact with kami, Bud-dhas, and ancestors. As important as it has been, the home is not sacred in isolation from the rest of the world; rather, the home is reinforced and complemented by other sacred space.

In every area of Japan there are a number of sacred sites outside the home. In the traditional village, two of the key sacred sites are the Shinto shrine of the tutelary kami and the Buddhist parish tem-ple. In a small community there may be only one tutelary shrine, whereas in a village there are usually several tutelary shrines, each with its own area and its own families. Traditionally, families went to the tutelary shrine during annual festivals to come into more di-rect contact with the local tutelary kami; often the custom was to bring home a printed shrine paper as the physical symbol of the kami's protective blessing. This practice makes clear that the shrine of the tutelary kami is a special sacred space in the village able to "charge" the homes of its territory with sacredness through contact with worshipers and distribution of its shrine papers. Families paid visits to the tutelary shrine at crucial junctures in life: the first time a child was taken out of the home was when it was carried to the tutelary shrine and placed under the protective care of the tutelary kami.

The Buddhist parish temple has a double sacred character, some-what like the butsudan in the home, because it enshrines both Bud-dhas and ancestors. Buddhist statues dominate the altar of a parish

Buddhist temple; formal ceremonies are held before the Buddhas, and individuals may revere the Buddhas there from time to time. But from a popular point of view, the sacredness of the parish temple comes mainly from the family ancestors whose ashes are enshrined there. Usually a funeral mass is performed in the parish temple, and memorial observances are carried out both informally in the home and more formally in the parish temple. Since Tokugawa times, cemeteries have been located next to parish temples; these "cemeteries" are actually places for erecting memorial stones (rather than for burying bodies). Family members make annual or more frequent visits to the memorial stones of their ancestors and may offer flowers and incense. These parish temple cemeteries are crowded with people during the late summer festival of the dead; if at all possible, a person will visit the family memorial stone at this time, even if it means traveling hundreds of miles. The two busiest times of travel in Japan are at the New Year and during the late summer festival of the dead, when people leave cities and return to their "home villages."

The parish Buddhist temple represents a sacred space somewhat different from that of the tutelary shrine. The parish temple is more closely related to the blessing of ancestors (through a social tie), providing blessings for families that have a hereditary relationship to this temple; the tutelary shrine is more directly related to kami of the local scene (through a residential tie), providing protection for homes located within this area. But there is a similarity in the relationship of both parish temple and tutelary shrine to the home: in both cases the space and character of the home are "charged" or reinforced by the power or sacredness of a sacred space outside it. The tutelary shrine makes it possible for a home to enshrine the tutelary kami annually. The parish temple helps sanctify the home memorial tablets in two ways: it ritually transforms the dead person into a benevolent ancestor through a funeral mass, and it maintains the blessings of ancestors through enshrining the ashes of the ancestors and performing memorials for them.

Just as the traditional home defined a sacred space of its own, the traditional village marked off a territory with its own sacred space. A village had boundary deities at the major entrance to the village, in effect, helping sanctify and protect the village against any evil force attempting to enter; villagers going on pilgrimage were sent off and welcomed back at this sacred threshold of the village. The traditional village also included other sacred sites, such as small chapels for specific Buddhas and small shrines for particular kami. Around the village there might have been a small waterfall, a hill, or a tree that according to local legend was the scene of some appearance of a kami or Buddha and was therefore considered a sacred site. Every village had its own pattern of sacred space made up of these different possibilities. As traditions and villages have changed, many of these practices have been discontinued, but there are still many small sacred spaces, even in contemporary Japanese cities. It is impossible to walk down the side streets of Tokyo without passing many small chapels and shrines. Most of the commuters and shoppers rush by these chapels and shrines, but the presence of fresh offerings indicates that some people continue to pay respects there. And the larger shrines and temples of major cities are thronged on such occasions as the New Year.

There are sacred sites outside both the home and the village (or

A Shinto shrine within the national headquarters of the New Religion Gedatsu-kai; this headquarters is called goreichi, *literally, "sacred land." The woman walking up the path toward the shrine has just purified her hands and mouth with water (at a site to the left of the path, not seen in the photograph) and is passing through the* torii *or sacred archway. She proceeds to the front of the shrine, where she will make an offering of money and bow her head in prayer. This setting is typical of many local Shinto shrines.*

This view from the front of a large Tokyo temple toward the entrance gate in the background shows the number of people who visit such temples. After entering the temple gate, each person follows his or her interest — admiring the old buildings, buying fortune papers or protective charms, buying and burning incense (especially for spirits of the dead; note the smoke rising in the upper part of the picture), and entering the temple itself for offerings of money and brief prayers.

city neighborhood), in regional or special sacred locations. Some of these are larger versions of the Shinto shrines and Buddhist temples in the local setting, providing special power and protection. For example, large Shinto shrines and Buddhist temples along the seacoast may "specialize" in praying for good fishing, protection on the sea, and repose of the souls of those who have drowned. A large shrine or temple may have a good reputation for providing a particular blessing, and individuals or groups may visit there to obtain that blessing. Several sacred mountains are famous as good places to memorialize ancestors (the spirits of the dead may be memorialized in any number of sacred places); families from several hundred square miles around such a sacred mountain travel there, sometimes taking a portion of the ashes or an article belonging to the dead person to be part of the memorializing ritual.

Some sacred centers can be considered both regional and national. For example, the headquarters of Buddhist denominations often have a special quality, for a number of reasons: they are the places where founders of the denomination (holy persons) lived and worked; they are rich in history and local tradition; and they are favorite sites for families to memorialize their ancestors. Going to such a headquarters means coming into contact with the benefit of a holy person as well as the other traditions and the ancestors. Such headquarters are popular places for pilgrimage, especially for families whose parish temple belongs to that headquarters; families or groups of families travel to a headquarters and stay in temple buildings, attending special services honoring ancestors (and possibly participating in other devotional practices). In one respect, memorializing one's ancestor at a headquarters temple can be considered a level above services at the local parish temple and in the home. This makes the headquarters temple like a national center, but it can also be like a regional center if people of the surrounding area go there to come into contact with objects of worship associated with local legend. (The headquarters of New Religions represent another complex example of sacred space: they are sites of nationwide pilgrimage, making them a kind of "national" center, but only for the members of that New Religion.)

On the highest level, the religious organization of space in Japan makes the land itself a kind of sacred space. We have seen that Japan as a nation or political entity is a kind of sacred group of people; here we are looking at Japan as the land and physical space. From ancient times there has been the mythological tradition of the Japanese islands having been created by kami, and many local traditions of sacred space dedicated to kami are variations of this nationwide theme that Japan is the "land of the kami." The hundreds of sacred mountains in Japan, from the majestic Mount Fuji to the hill of the local village, are all examples of the land of Japan being filled with the presence of kami. The presence of many Buddhas in Japan is a reinforcement of this theme, for the popular notion is not of imported Buddhas but Buddhas who appeared in particular Japanese locations for the benefit of the local people.

Traditionally, one of the most sacred spots in Japan as a national center has been the Ise Shrine, since it enshrines the Sun Goddess, from whom the imperial line descended. Since medieval times people have made pilgrimages there to come into contact with the power that founded the nation. Several other shrines associated with emperors and traditional notions of the founding of Japan became important during the last hundred years, when Japan developed as a more centralized nation-state.

Another key shrine that has become part of the constitutional controversy over "national" shrines is the Yasukuni Shrine. During the past century, this shrine in Tokyo became the central site for enshrining the spirits of soldiers and sailors who died while on duty. One of the spiritual advantages of being enshrined at the Yasukuni Shrine is that, because these military men died while carrying out their loyalty to the emperor and nation, their spirits are directly associated with the spirits of past emperors. This direct contact with imperial ancestors is not possible for other people in Japanese society. Whatever one thinks about the constitutional issue (which revolves around national financing of a particular religion and the potential for encouragement of militarism), obviously the Yasukuni Shrine is a prime example of "national" sacred space.

The cities of Kyoto and Nara, both former capitals of Japan, also represent sacred space, because they are the places where so much of Japanese history was acted out. These two capitals are full of major shrines and temples and are extremely popular for both pilgrimage and tourism. Many of the shrines and temples are designated by the government as "national treasures" or "important cultural treasures" because of their historic significance, and some state funds are used to finance the restoration and maintenance of the buildings (but not any rituals). When Japanese people visit these capitals— whether as individuals, families, or busloads of schoolchildren— even if they do not participate in specific religious ceremonies, they are coming into contact with the national heritage, and this makes the capitals part of the national tradition of sacred space. These two capitals are the best examples, but there are shrines and temples outside Kyoto and Nara designated "national treasures" that also qualify as part of the national organization of religious space.

The where of religious organization in Japan is extremely varied, with sacred space in the home and village as well as regional and national space. This is quite different from modern Western countries where sacred space is most often limited to religious buildings. Because sacred space is so widespread in Japan, the question arises whether all space in Japan is sacred. It would be an exaggeration to say that the entire land space of Japan is sacred, but in contrast to modern Western countries, the religious organization of space in Japan is much more diffuse and expressed in a greater variety of forms. From the local scene of home and village to the larger scene of regional and national sacred centers, living in relation to these sacred spaces helps the Japanese people define their sense of place in the world—in other words, the religious world of space.

The Religious World of Time

The when of religious organization is the arrangement of religious events through time in a regular sequence, usually an annual pattern. Every religion has some kind of calendar that it follows to enact through time the religious ideals that it treasures. By acting out these ideals through time, not only is the message preserved and celebrated, but individuals and the community "realize" the message in their own lives. By participating in the rhythm of the annual celebrations, a person's life is regulated or organized into a meaningful rhythm. The religious world of time is this process of ordering religious events in a repeated annual sequence for all members of a community so that their participation in these events conforms to a set of religious ideals.

In a monotheistic religion like Christianity, the "church year" or "liturgical year" is oriented around the worship of God. In churches emphasizing liturgical worship, such as the Roman Catholic and Protestant Episcopal Churches, the liturgy is printed in book form (the Missal for the Roman Catholic Church and the Book of Common Prayer for the Protestant Episcopal Church) and followed closely in regular worship services. (American Christians also participate in popular festivals of a religious or semireligious nature, such as Memorial Day and Thanksgiving, but ordinarily they do not consider them as part of the church year.)

In Japanese religion, too, the religious organization of time is closely related to objects of worship, especially kami and ancestors. But the timing of annual events in Japanese religion presents two sharp contrasts with the liturgical year of Christianity: first, the Japanese religious year is not determined by just one religion but is regulated by several religious traditions; second, the Japanese religious year is more diffuse, corresponding more to the seasons, and depends more on custom and oral tradition than on a single liturgical book. In Japanese there is a general term, *nenju gyoji*, or "annual religious events," that refers to the ceremonies or events observed by all the people of an area on a certain day every year. In traditional Japan the day of an annual event was set apart from ordinary days by particular behavior, such as refraining from work (because in order to participate in the event one had to be "pure"). Every person or family in a traditional village was expected to participate in these annual events. Each village or region had some distinctive festivals or practices (for example, a seaside area would hold an annual harbor festival), but many annual events have been observed throughout Japan. Today some of these events are still held as religious festivals; others are seen more as days of recreation and times for the preparing of special foods.

Before treating the actual festivals, it is necessary to explain some of the general principles of time reckoning in Japan, for there are three kinds of calendars that help detemine the dates for festivals. The calendar most Westerners use, the solar calendar of 365 days and twelve months (the Gregorian calendar, which also features a leap year), has been adopted in modern Japan and is used to determine many annual events: for example, by the solar calendar, New Year's Day is January 1. A second form of calendar used in Japan is the lunar calendar, following the twenty-eight-day cycle of the moon. Some festivals are held on the first day of the lunar calendar (the new moon), others, on the fifteenth day of the lunar calendar (the full moon). The lunar calendar begins with the first lunar month of twenty-eight days after the winter solstice. For example, one special New Year celebration was held traditionally on the first full moon following the winter solstice. (Just as the date of Easter in Christian countries varies each year according to the lunar patterns, so the date of these lunar festivals in Japan will not fall on the same day of the solar calendar every year).

A third form of calendar is the Chinese almanac, which was adopted by the Japanese so long ago that it has become part of Japanese tradition. The Chinese calendar is regulated by the rotation of two interlocking patterns: ten heavenly "stems" and twelve earthly "branches," which form a repeating cycle of sixty units. This is applied especially to days, and each day can be identified by the intersection of a stem and a branch within this sixty-day cycle. This calendar is used to designate some festivals and may also be consulted generally for lucky and unlucky days and for a personal horoscope. (New almanacs are printed every year and bought in large numbers by people who use them to follow festivals, lucky days, and personal fortunes.)

There are so many annual religious events in Japan that it is not possible to mention all of them. In fact, Japanese folklorists write whole books on the annual events of just one region, to record its particular practices. In this brief interpretation we will only highlight some of the major annual events observed throughout Japan, giving their names, dates of celebration, and general significance. We will start with a description of the New Year and then identify other major annual events through the course of a year.

The New Year is one of the most important and most widely celebrated annual events in Japan. As in other cultures, this time marks the end of one year and the beginning of another, but in Japan the celebration spans several weeks. Preparation begins in late December, when people clean their homes to purify them in readiness for the coming of the ancestors; also at the end of December, Shinto shrines perform a "great purification" rite to rid people of impurities and defilements from the previous half year. The New Year itself is very important both for homes and for shrines and temples. After the home is cleaned, a pine branch may be placed on the house gate and a rope made of rice straw hung over the entrance: both indicate renewal and sacred space. Inside the house a special altar (in addition to the kamidana and butsudan) is set up: in agricultural areas this may be seen as welcoming the rice kami; elsewhere it is seen as a welcoming of the ancestors.

People make their first visit of the year to shrines and temples late on New Year's Eve or on New Year's Day, as a lucky way of beginning the year. Huge crowds of people throng the shrines and temples, making small offerings of money and saying prayers for blessing in the coming year. For good measure, a fortune paper can be bought for a small sum, often from a vending machine; the fortune paper may predict good luck, or tell how to avoid bad luck. People also replace some shrine papers in the home at this time, bringing old papers with them to the shrine, throwing them away (often burning them), and buying new ones. The belief is that the old shrine papers have absorbed bad luck and illness during the year, protecting the family against this bad fortune; now they are used up and need to be replaced. There is another celebration called the Little New Year, falling on the first full moon of the new year (about January 15); although technically a separate festival, it is an extension of the New Year festivities. The highlight of this event is a bonfire at night; in some areas this is when old shrine papers and temple papers are burned. Generally this bonfire is a celebtation greeting the kami of rice and seeking a plentiful and profitable new year.

The significance of this New Year celebration is almost as broad as Japanese religion itself. It is a replacement of impurity with purity. It is also a means by which humans establish a new beginning in harmony with the new beginning of nature. People purify their homes and give a special welcome to ancestors; they visit shrines and temples to come into contact with kami and Buddhas, to start the year with sacredness and power. All these practices and beliefs demonstrate how crucial the New Year is, an excellent start for making human time conform to religious time.

The next annual event we look at is the "change of seasons" celebrated on February 3, considered the last day of winter but also the opening of spring. This is another day that has been set aside for the driving out of evil and impurity. The festival has become associated with the throwing of soybeans. When it is celebrated at home, soybeans are thrown out of the house to expel evil and thrown into the house to bring in good luck. It is still a popular festival today, usually held at shrines and temples; children try to gather the soybeans thrown into a crowd as a sign of good luck for the year. This annual event is another means of marking the passage of the seasons, driving out impurities, and seeking good luck.

The doll festival, held March 3, is the second annual event that corresponds to a set of five Chinese festivals borrowed in ancient times and now completely adapted to Japanese customs. The Chinese way of reckoning these festivals is the first day of the first month (New Year's Day), the third day of the third month (the doll festival), the fifth day of the fifth month (boys' day), the seventh day of the seventh month (the star festival), and the ninth day of the ninth month (the chrysanthemum festival). The New Year celebration in Japan is so elaborate that the Chinese precedent is largely forgotten. The doll festival today is especially for girls, who arrange an elaborate display of dolls in the home. Nowadays the festival is mainly recreation for girls (and big business for department stores, which sell very expensive dolls); but in earlier times, paper dolls were used and thrown away into streams to carry away the impurities of the people. The doll festival may once have signified purification, but today it is mainly a day of relaxation and recreation.

The spring festival for the tutelary kami is celebrated according to the Chinese-style almanac on a day close to the spring equinox. People within the area of a tutelary kami pay visits to the tutelary shrine to make offerings and pray for the kami's blessing. This annual event signifies the asking of protection from the tutelary kami, but at the same time it is celebrated according to a seasonal rhythm that links both humans and kami and home and shrine to the rhythm of nature.

The spring equinox, celebrated during the week of the spring equinox (March 23), is associated with Buddhism and ancestors. The term *equinox* in Japanese, *higan*, also means "the other shore," referring to both death and the Buddhist goal of nirvana, or enlightenment. During this time, it is customary for people to return to their hometowns and honor family ancestors with offerings and visits to memorial stones. This annual event is another in the series of ceremonies centering on the blessing of ancestors.

The flower festival, falling on April 8, has been associated with various practices. It was widely regarded as the day when mountain kami descended, entered the rice fields, and became rice kami for the growing season, returning to the mountains in the fall. People climbed mountains and brought flowers from the mountain to their homes or rice fields, symbolizing the movement of kami (which were also associated with ancestral spirits). People still celebrate this day by having picnics on nearby mountains or hills and picking wild flowers. This festival signifies the coming of spring and the bounty of nature, which in this case is associated both with local kami and the blessings of ancestors. (April 8 is also the day the Japanese observe as the birthday of the historical Buddha, and temples perform a special ritual pouring sweet tea over a small statue of the infant Buddha.)

Boys' day, on May 5, is the third in the set of five Chinese festivals. The earlier purpose of this summer festival may have been to drive away evil spirits with dolls dressed as soldiers and placed outside the house gate. Later, the festival became more of a celebration of the growth and strength of boys, who arranged a display of miniature warriors in the home. Like the doll festival on March 3, boys' day has become mainly a form of recreation for children, and the miniature warriors that boys display may be just as expensive as the dolls bought by girls for the doll festival. A distinctive decoration of boys' day is a cloth streamer fashioned in the shape of a carp and hung from a pole to wave in the wind. Carp are symbolic of strength and vitality, and parents exhibit the streamers to celebrate and encourage strength in young boys.

The great purification falls on June 30, in a month full of other observances emphasizing avoidance of impurities. The great purification is performed at local tutelary shrines, with the purpose of destroying all the impurities the people of the shrine's area have accumulated since New Year's Day. Sometimes people take to the shrine a simple paper doll that they have rubbed against their bodies, thus symbolizing the transfer of impurities to the doll, which is left at the tutelary shrine and disposed of by Shinto priests. This great purification ceremony complements the same ceremony at year's end (preparing for the New Year): both are means of periodically purifying life and bringing it into harmony with the sacredness of kami generally, especially the tutelary kami.

The star festival is held July 7, another in the set of five Chinese festivals. It is called the star festival because, according to tradition, a weaver and her lover became stars and are able to meet only on this day. Traditionally, people celebrated this annual meeting of the stars representing the lovers by writing poems on colored papers and hanging them from bamboo poles. One of the benefits prayed for was greater facility in writing and crafts. In modern times some cities have made the star festival a major commercial undertaking, with entire city blocks elaborately decorated. Stores compete with one another to exhibit the largest and prettiest decorations in the streets in front of the stores. This festival, like others, has become more recreation and relaxation than religious ritual.

The festival of the dead, July 13–16, is seen as a Buddhist event, but it is related completely to the ancestors. Spirits of the ancestors are welcomed in the home with special offerings. Families visit the memorial stones for ancestors and clean the area, often pouring water over the memorial stone. At this time of the year, the family may also pay a Buddhist priest to come to the home and recite a Buddhist scripture in front of the butsudan. Villages or city neighborhoods may arrange folk dances with a small musical group as a communal way of welcoming the presence of the ancestors. In traditional times there were colorful practices of greeting and sending off the ancestors, such as building small fires outside the gate to the house. The significance of the festival of the dead is greater than can be indicated in this brief description—in terms of the annual round of events, it is comparable in importance to the New Year, because it is the most important occasion for honoring the family ancestors.

The fall festival for the tutelary kami is the counterpart of the spring festival for the tutelary kami; the fall festival is held according to the Chinese almanac on a day close to the fall equinox, September 23. The fall practices mirror those in spring; people of a given area visit the shrine of their tutelary kami with simple offerings and prayers. The fall festival again signifies asking protection from the tutelary kami and keeping in harmony people and nature, home and shrine. During the fall there are also many rituals marking the harvest of rice, usually a kind of thanksgiving ceremony. Harvest festivals are performed according to the lunar calendar but vary considerably due to the difference in climate from north to south and the ripening of rice from about August to November. Traditionally, this is the time when the kami of the rice fields return to the mountains, becoming the mountain kami once more; this balances the flower festival of April 8.

The fall *higan*, or "equinox," is celebrated for a week at the time of the fall equinox, September 23. This is the counterpart of the spring equinox, when again people visit family memorial stones and honor their ancestors. The significance of the fall higan, as of the spring, is to honor the ancestors and receive their blessings.

December ends the year with the preparation for the New Year, as has been indicated, with the celebration of the great purification that takes care of impurities accumulated from June 30 to the end of the year. This brings to a close the year's major annual religious events.[6]

The when of religious organization in Japan is a sequence of rituals and festivals that is repeated in the same fashion year after year. The strength of repetition in religion lies in its reinforcement of the power of the sacred model that it imitates. Just as the liturgical year of a Roman Catholic or Protestant Episcopal church repeats the same ritual pattern annually, drawing on the power of God, so the rhythm of annual events in Japan draws on the power of kami, Buddhas, and ancestors. The most important ritual events are emphasized by their being represented twice in the annual round. Major purification rituals come at year's end and midyear. Ancestors are prominent in the home at the New Year and during the festival for the dead; also formal respects are paid to them during the spring and fall equinox celebrations. The tutelary kami is visited especially during spring and fall. Agricultural rhythms of spring and fall balance planting and harvesting with welcoming and sending off the mountain kami and rice field kami. Japanese religion organizes time in a regular schedule of events, so that human time can correspond to sacred time. The religious ideals of living in close relation to kami, Buddhas, and ancestors are realized in the lives of people by acting out these ideals through the passage of time. This orderly pattern of annual events creates a religious world of time according to which people can regulate their lives with assurance of power and blessing.

The Religious World of Human Life

The how of the religious world is the way in which religion is related to the course of human life. A person is born, matures, and dies, passing through a series of biological stages; but religion helps organize life into successive steps in the realization of a meaningful career. This career roughly follows biological states, but religious rituals have their own way of defining the stages and adding meaning to them. In the previous section, we viewed the religious organization of time as a series of annual events repeated in the span of a year for all or most people. Now we look at the religious organization of human activities as the cycle of life followed by an individual. One means of tracing the life cycle in any culture is to describe the religious rituals and observances that occur from birth to death— "from cradle to grave." After tracing the life cycle, other religious practices will be mentioned that an individual may use to enhance his or her spiritual experience.

In traditional Japan there were many rituals related to the life cycle, not all of which are practiced today. In modern Japan some religious and semireligious customs have come to be practiced in addition to, or replacing, the traditional rituals. In this brief overview we will cite some of the more important traditional rituals as well as some more recent customs, indicating the life stage, the practices associated with it, and its religious significance.

The first life stage is birth, which, in Japan, as in most cultures, is associated with various rituals. In traditional Japan there were many taboos or avoidances associated with birth, which was considered impure partly because of the blood involved. In former times a woman even gave birth and lived for a short while with her newborn child in a special isolation hut built for this purpose; it was important for the new mother to cook her food on a separate fire in order not to defile the rest of the family. Such practices have long disappeared in Japan, but some traces remain (as seen in the infant's first trip outside of the home).

When a child is born, it is given a soul or spirit by a birth kami, which once was considered separate from the tutelary kami but today is thought to be the same. A month after birth the taboos associated with birth end; in other words, the child is free from birth impurities and is taken by its parents to the shrine of the tutelary kami. Traditionally, the infant's first trip outside the home was when it was carried to the shrine of the tutelary kami. (This trip is comparable to christening in a Christian setting.) The traditional interpretation of the baby being presented to the tutelary kami is that the baby is (or becomes) the child of the tutelary kami. The individual has a special relationship to the tutelary kami: he or she should, for example, participate in the annual festivals at the tutelary shrine. This individual worships at the shrine of the tutelary kami, who protects him or her. Birth rituals usher the infant into life by affirming the source of life as the kami and by establishing a relationship between child and kami.

As medical facilities have advanced and birth takes place in modern hospitals, many of the traditions surrounding birth have disappeared. But some traditional practices survive even in a modern hospital. For example, there is a rich folklore related to the umbilical cord, which was preserved at birth and treasured. Later in life the cord was used to help a person recover from sickness. In some regions it was buried with the mother who bore the child, or it could be buried with the person to whom it belonged. Some modern hospitals still save the umbilical cord for parents; when my son was born in Japan in 1963, the hospital presented us with his umbilical cord in a camphor wood box.

The family has special celebrations for the child associated both with the growth of the child and the child's entrance into annual events. On the first birthday, there is a special celebration. Also, there is a special celebration for the child's first participation in the doll festival (for girls) or in the boys' festival. A particular festival observed for children of both sexes occurs in the third, fifth, and seventh years: girls participate at ages three and seven, boys only at age five. This annual festival is held November 15 and is named Shichigosan, literally, "seven-five-three," after the ages of children attending the festival. Children dress up in their finest clothes and visit their tutelary shrine. The purpose of these visits is to pray to the tutelary kami to protect them as they grow and mature. In other words, growth is not simply a biological matter but a process nurtured and protected by kami and other spiritual powers.

There are a number of rites that traditionally marked the passage of children into the status of young men and women or, later, adults. In some areas young men had their own associations, which they entered in their teens and left at marriage. Such associations have long ceased, but even today the point at which a young man first participates in a local festival, especially in the carrying of a portable altar around the shrine's territory, is a kind of "coming of age" event. In traditional Japan there was a collective ritual for teenage boys marking their adolescence with the granting of a loincloth. Adolescence for girls was celebrated individually after the first menstruation, marked by the granting of an underskirt. Such practices, which feature religious and social recognition of growth and sexual maturity, are no longer observed.

Today there is a national holiday on January 15, an official coming of age for all young men and women who will become twenty during that year. The present practice has a legal aspect, since these young people are now adults and can marry without parental consent. Another modern style of initiation is the ceremony admitting young people into the employment of a large company, which includes formalities similar to adoption into a family, or becoming the "child" of the company (comparable to becoming the child of the tutelary kami).

A special religious aid for coping with life in modern Japan is the custom of praying at certain Shinto shrines famous for help in passing college entrance examinations. Before and at the time of examination, both mothers of students and the young people taking the examination may visit such shrines. Getting into a good university is crucial for securing a prestigious job, arranging a favorable marriage, and generally doing well in life, so the applicant can use all the help he or she can get. Of course the student has to study hard, but this is an extra step to help one pass through the examination successfully. This is a good illustration of how new rites arise even as old ones die out.

Marriages traditionally occurred in the home, and the crucial ceremony was the ritual exchange of sake (rice wine) between the bride and groom. Every locale had its own set of wedding customs. In many cases, the marriage was held in front of the butsudan, or at least the marriage was announced to the ancestors in the butsudan. No priest was needed for this traditional wedding, which was essentially an agreement between families. In recent times, weddings have become more formal and more expensive. During the past century there has arisen the custom of "marriage before the kami," in other words, a marriage in a Shinto shrine. Some large shrines with beautiful grounds are popular as wedding sites and make considerable money from this business. Commercial wedding halls are also rented for this purpose. Very formal dress is required for weddings, either formal Japanese dress (kimono) or maybe a tuxedo for the groom and a Western-style wedding dress for the bride. "Christian"-style weddings have had considerable influence in Japan, even though very few Japanese are members of Christian churches. A marriage obviously is a ritual joining two lives, but in Japan this has meant even more—the joining of two families. Some traditional practices have largely passed away, taken over by the new customs developed at Shinto shrines and even commercial wedding halls. This is symptomatic of some of the secular tendencies in modern Japan. But tradition lives on, and the Chinese almanac is still a factor in determining a favorable day for a wedding (or a funeral).

As a person grows older, there are specific years of danger and years of celebration. Every person can consult the almanac to watch for times of good luck and bad luck, but the most dangerous age for men is forty-two, for women, thirty-three. During this year of life a person should take pains to avoid any evil forces and, to counteract danger, should participate more actively in shrine festivals. Two years celebrated as auspicious are the sixty-first, since it begins the first year after a sixty-year cycle (according to the traditional almanac), and the seventieth, seen as a rare achievement. These notions reinforce the general understanding that life is not a simple biological continuity but has its bad times and good times. The almanac and related practices help the individual minimize or avoid bad times and maximize good times.

Rites for the dead are the last stage in this cradle-to-grave cycle, but in Japan the afterlife is more complicated than it is in Western countries. As we have seen in the treatment of ancestors, a person has a long "career" even after death, beginning with the funeral ceremony. In traditional times, there were many customs involved with the preparation of the body for the funeral; the general notion is that the soul leaves the body at death and must be prepared for the next world. For example, it was customary to place a bowl of rice by the body to help sustain the person in the next life and a sharp instrument to protect against evil spirits. In village settings members of the village cooperated to help prepare the body for the funeral, including washing the body, clothing it in white, and placing it in a coffin. The corpse is considered impure, and these preparatory acts, as well as the funeral and memorial rites, are intended to purify the body. The funeral service is conducted by Buddhist priests, who recite Buddhist scriptures, after which all accompany the body to the burial ground or crematorium. In modern times many of the preparations tend to be handled by undertakers.

The general principles and practices for the transformation of the spirit of the dead person into an ancestor continue today, with some variations, depending on the Buddhist sect with which the person's family is affiliated. Usually the Buddhist posthumous name is granted by a Buddhist priest at the time of the funeral and written on a temporary memorial tablet, which is taken home from the funeral and set up in front of the butsudan. For forty-nine days, the family is in mourning, and it was formerly the custom for families not to visit or interact with other families during this time of mourning and taboo. (The forty-nine days also correspond to the time some Buddhist texts claim is required for a person to travel through purgatory). The forty-ninth day signifies the completion of the purification of the dead person and his or her transformation into an ancestral spirit. At that time the temporary memorial tablet is removed, and a permanent memorial tablet is placed in the butsudan. Thereafter, memorial masses are held on the first anniversary of death and at regular intervals, especially on the annual anniversary of the death day, often ending with the thirty-third anniversary. The final memorial mass for the ancestor is significant, because it marks the end of the individual identity of the ancestral spirit; it then joins the "generations of ancestors."

The general belief is that as ancestral spirits lose their individual identity they merge with the ancestral kami of the family. In fact, it is felt that this vague group of ancestral family kami is responsible for birth, and an ancestral spirit may be reborn in the form of a baby born to the family. Japanese death rituals have much in common with death rituals throughout the world, which ease the transition from death and impurity to a new life. What is distinctive about the Japanese practice is the rather prolonged series of rituals after death and the strong association of spirits of the dead with the benefit of the ongoing family. It is interesting to note that death rituals actually circle back to birth, showing how the life cycle is complete and repeats itself in the career of individuals.

Just as the series of annual events is repeated on a yearly basis in the lives of all people, so the cycle is repeated for each individual through the life span. A person learns this cycle of life not by formal teachings, but by viewing other people pass through ritual events such as birth, marriage, and death; at the same time, a person is living out his or her career by passing through these life stages and rituals as they appear. In this fashion, the religious organization of life provides a spiritual blueprint by which people can plan and act out their lives in the attempt to fulfill the religious ideal: in Japan the ideal is to live a full and meaningful life in relation to kami and Buddhas, eventually becoming an ancestor and even a form of kami.

In addition to the rhythmic pattern of rituals from cradle to grave, there are many religious activities in which an individual can participate as an individual, rather than as part of a group. We have seen that usually the individual participates in religion through social groups such as the family, village, and nation. But as an individual a person has various other alternatives. One possibility already mentioned is the almanac, which includes predictions for individuals based on such personal variables as birthdate. Also, anyone who experiences a personal problem may consult a fortune-teller or buy a fortune paper at a shrine or temple. As in Western countries, often horoscopes and fortune-telling are criticized as "superstitious" and joked about, but their popularity (and the abundance of printed material throughout the world) demonstrates the conscious and unconscious importance of such beliefs. Many traditional beliefs continue in modern Japan and influence individuals in their daily life.

Some individual practices might be considered devotional, such as recitation of a devotional phrase (the nembutsu, for example, placing faith in Amida). A family member may participate in simple offerings and prayers before the butsudan, but many also recite a part of a Buddhist scripture individually as a personal devotion before the butsudan. Most of the beliefs and practices of Japanese religion described in this chapter have to do with collective activity, but there is also room for individual conscience and action. Anyone who feels that he or she has done something wrong may go to a shrine, such as the tutelary shrine, to apologize to the tutelary kami, or pay a visit to a temple and recite a simple repentance. A typical case is when the individual feels "unfilial"—lacking in reverence to parents and ancestors—or thinks he or she is the cause of disharmony in the family. In this case a person may "apologize," or repent. A stronger form of this practice is the "hundredfold" repentance, called in Japanese *ohyakudo*, literally, "a hundred times." Some shrines and temples have a set of two stone markers for practicing this form of repentance within their precincts, and the conscience-stricken individual walks back and forth a hundred times between the two stones (usually barefoot) reciting repentance.

More rigorous forms of practice depend on the individual's degree of religious commitment and the seriousness of the religious request. For example, a common means of intensifying religious commitment has been to make a pilgrimage to a sacred center, such as the Ise Shrine, or a regional sacred center. During World War II, one or both parents might fulfill a vow to visit a hundred shrines as a prayer of protection for a son in the war. Even today, people who wish to deepen their spiritual life may make a personal vow to visit a local shrine or temple a certain number of times, usually for early morning prayers. The individual gets up early (in traditional times the person might take a cold water shower as an ascetic practice to show strength of purpose), goes to the nearby shrine and says a simple prayer, and returns home or goes to work.

One of the common ways of advancing spiritually is to "study" religion, meaning to read popular books about Buddhism or Buddhist scriptures or to read explanations of doctrine distributed by denominations or New Religions. Popular books on religion sell very well in Japanese bookstores, and it is no accident that many New Religions got their start through publishing and still maintain sophisticated publishing facilities.

Another form of individual practice is meditation. Usually meditation is practiced in a group, and it is rare for a person to leave home and become a Zen monk or nun meditating full-time. But even New Religions have simple techniques for meditation—sitting quietly in a formal posture and purifying the mind while thinking of one's own defects and concentrating on an object of worship. Usually these techniques are practiced in joint meetings, but they may be repeated at home individually, as part of daily devotions.

These two means of organizing religious life—from cradle to grave, and by individual practice—show how Japanese religion is related to the flow of the human career and the meeting of personal problems. Life is more than mere biological development, it is the acting out of a drama of spiritual fulfillment with roles played by both human beings and objects of worship. A person is able to chart where he or she is in the life cycle by participating in the rituals for other people and by checking off his or her own ritual landmarks through life. If a particular problem arises, there are beliefs and practices to correct one's mistakes and deepen one's spirituality. All these practices—both the cycle from cradle to grave, and individual devotions—help an individual construct his or her own religious world of human life as a plan for spiritual fulfillment.

We have now viewed representative aspects and examples of the smaller "worlds" of Japanese religion, looking first at four kinds of objects of worship, and then surveying the religious significance of society, space, time, and human life. This selective treatment is intended to provide an interpretation of the nature of Japanese religion as a unified world view. Each of these smaller worlds represents a unity of one aspect of religion and one dimension of religious practice. All these subworlds or smaller worlds of religion and dimen-

sions of religious practice contribute to the total religious world view
in Japan, what we have called "one sacred way." This sacred way is
not just a particular place or a specific building or an organized institution—it is the total understanding of the universe and how a human career can be lived meaningfully within it. Each "world"
brings into order one aspect of this world view or universe of meaning. These worlds are not separate entities but interlocking parts of
this sacred way that is the implicit religious system at the heart of
Japanese religious life.

■

CHAPTER V

The Dynamics of
Japanese Religion

In this chapter Japanese religion will be presented more concretely and specifically. The previous chapters have provided overviews that help us better understand the Japanese religious heritage as a whole. Unfortunately, such generalizations may leave the false impression that Japanese religion is a dry historical framework or an abstract system. However, any religious tradition is much more than its recorded historical development or its implied systematic organization. When people actually participate in and experience religion, it is rich in detail and drama. Even as an "outsider" to Japanese religion, I have always been fascinated by and caught up in the human and spiritual drama of the festivals I have observed and the lives of people who have talked to me about their experiences. In previous chapters it has only been possible to give brief examples and illustrations that hint at the vitality of Japanese religion as it is acted out in actual lives and concrete events. The present chapter focuses on this concrete aspect—the "dynamics" of Japanese religion as it is acted out and experienced by Japanese people.

Two examples of religious dynamics that I have studied personally have been selected for description and discussion. From more than twenty years of studying Japanese religion, these examples stand out as interesting documents of important aspects of religious life today. The first is a village festival celebrating this rural community's religious welcoming of spring. The second is the life history of a Tokyo man who is a member of a New Religion. These examples cover much of the range of Japanese religion, from village to me-

tropolis, from performance of a traditional festival to participation
in a New Religion. Each example will be introduced briefly, described at greater length, and then interpreted in the context of Japanese religion as a whole.

The Spring Mountain Festival

Village festivals, in which all or most of the community participate,
have been some of the most important annual events for the Japanese during the past few hundred years. These festivals are still held
in some regions, even though their contemporary form is modified
and shortened. One example of such a village festival is the *haru-
yama*, or "spring mountain," festival carried out by the people in
the village of Toge in Yamagata Prefecture (in northeastern Honshu, facing the Sea of Japan). During the celebration of spring
mountain, representatives of the village climb a nearby mountain
and symbolically welcome spring by bringing the mountain kami
down to bless rice fields and homes.

Some knowledge about the village and local customs is necessary
for understanding the festival. In the area around Toge are three
sacred mountains—Haguro, Gassan, and Yudono. Each mountain
was believed to be the sacred abode of a mountain kami and a counterpart Buddhist divinity. (For Gassan the counterpart Buddha is
Amida.) From Tokugawa times, these three mountains were considered a triad of sacred mountains for gaining power through Buddhist ascetic practices. Before and during the Tokugawa period,
there were hundreds of sacred mountains throughout Japan where
the priests of Shugendo groups gained their training and exercised
their spiritual powers. Haguro, Gassan, and Yudono were known as
the three sacred mountains of Dewa, the traditional name for this
area. These mountains defined an important area of sacred space:
there was a great deal of religious activity both on the mountain and
between the mountains and the people of the surrounding area.
Shugendo priests gained their powers while training on the mountain and renewed these powers in ascetic practices on the mountain
every year. Priests left the mountain during parts of the year to travel
through specified territories to minister to the religious heads of the
people, providing prayers and rituals of all kinds, especially healing

rites. People from hundreds of square miles around made pilgrimages to these mountains, especially during the summer.

Toge has been a very important village in the practice of Shugendo at these three sacred mountains, as seen in the fact that the village once was the location of many of the combination lodging houses and temples to which Shugendo priests guided pilgrims on their way to these sacred mountains. The geographical location and name of the village at the foot of Mount Haguro are also clues to its religious significance. The name Toge is a variation of the word for "mountain pass," and in Japanese folk belief a mountain pass was considered an opening from this ordinary world into the special area of the sacred mountains. The village of Toge still retains traditional practices related to Shugendo and these sacred mountains.

Toge is a relatively small village with several hundred families. It is a farming village large enough to have its own small shops, post office, and school system up through grade school. Growing rice and other agricultural products was traditionally the most important economic activity. In more recent times there has been some logging around the mountains, but there is still no major industry. In Toge, as in all areas of Japan, farming has become less important than industrial production and services. Increasingly, men are drawn to work outside the community. The major nearby city is Tsuruoka, which has its own high school and also railway connections; there is regular bus service between Toge and Tsuruoka.

Toge has experienced the general shift of young men from farms to industrialized cities, but its own traditions and customs have not been so severely undermined as those in the more urbanized and industrialized areas. Toge is true to its rural setting by being relatively more traditional and conservative than urban Japan. Both Christianity and the highly successful New Religions have won very few members in Toge, which is an indication of the cohesiveness of the traditional practices in the village. The spring mountain is one of these traditional practices; it is described as I observed it in 1964.[7]

The spring mountain is a spring festival performed by representatives of Toge at the foot of Mount Haguro. The actual festival consists of two representatives (or proxies) from each of the eight **buraku**, or subdivisions, of Toge climbing Gassan (and perhaps making a round of the three sacred mountains) and bringing back to their respective buraku some mountain plants. The spring mountain was performed on the third, fourth, and fifth of May in 1964. (The date is actually determined by the "eighty-eighth night"—or day—after the beginning of spring according to the lunar calendar.) Early on the morning of May 3, the two men from each of the eight buraku who were proxies for that year's festival climbed from Toge, via a stone staircase, several miles to the Dewa Shrine at the summit of Mount Haguro. While climbing to the mountaintop shrine, respect was paid at the various smaller shrines along the way, by a nod of the head and clap of hands. Wearing the Shinto style of white surplice around their necks, they entered Dewa Shrine and were led in a simple prayer by a Shinto priest, after which they all received a small drink of sake from another Shinto priest. Then they met in a separate room and discussed the practical plans for carrying out the spring mountain. Since this was a village function, it was planned and carried out completely by the villagers and their buraku proxies.

On this morning, the villagers made some arrangements for lodging at the shrine's building, called Saikan ("Purification Hall"), the night of May 4 and decided to hire two trucks to take everyone as far as the "sixth station" of Gassan.[8] In earlier times it was the custom to walk to Gassan, but with the coming of modern transportation, all forms of pilgrimage have changed drastically. The notion of "stations" requires further explanation. The route for climbing many Japanese mountains, including Fuji, came to be divided into ten "stations," each station usually marked by a shrine or holy site. Probably this symbolism came from the Buddhist scheme of ten stages between hell and heaven; climbing a sacred mountain is analogous to traveling from hell to heaven, from profane to sacred.

After all the arrangements were completed at Dewa Shrine, tiny cups of sacred sake were passed around for a toast before the meeting broke up. Then everyone descended the stone staircase to Toge. On the way to Toge, the buraku proxies left the stone pathway and picked leaves of the evergreen camellia for members of their buraku. Camellia, they say, is about the same as Shinto's sacred plant sakaki, also an evergreen plant. In this case, taking the camellia leaves to the village represents the symbolic descent of the mountain kami to the village or rice field. This is a change from the pre–World War II practice of picking plants during the actual climb of

Gassan. After World War II, a large tract of land including most of the three mountains was made into a national park. The rules of the national park prohibit the removal of any plants or animals, thus making it impossible to bring back these plants from Gassan during the pilgrimage.

This morning trip took only several hours, and it was 9:30 A.M. when they returned to Toge. At this point the proxies went to their homes and awaited the truck ride to Gassan early the next morning. During the morning's activities, and throughout the spring mountain festival, these men obviously enjoyed themselves. They appreciated the break from their regular work, and as they climbed and descended the stone staircase, they chatted and joked with their friends. For special ceremonies, such as receiving sake from Shinto shrine priest, they were quiet and attentive. But at no point were the participants solemn or long-faced.

A clue to the whole ceremony of spring mountain is found in the name that all the proxies share. They are called *gyonin*, a word similar to *gyoja*, or "ascetic," which means that they are carrying out a special religious duty. Formerly there were more severe restrictions for these "ascetics," but even today they should observe religious abstinence. This means at least abstaining from meat and not cohabiting with one's wife during the time of the festival, including the preparation period preceding the festival. The white clothes traditionally worn by each ascetic, as well as the small white surplice, indicate the purity of his religious task.

On the morning of May 4, everyone gathered at 4:30 for the truck ride to Gassan. Men other than the proxies could participate voluntarily. A number of voluntary participants, an official ranger of the national forest (at the same time a member of the seventh buraku), and I increased the number of proxies from sixteen to just over thirty people. Crowded into two small trucks, all headed for Gassan, passing the road leading to the summit of Mount Haguro but not stopping at Dewa Shrina. The first stop was made about five o'clock at a small wayside shrine. This spot is called Daiman, technically the second station of Gassan. Everyone got out of the truck and gathered around the shrine to recite a simple prayer of purification. We then got back into the trucks, which began the rather steep ascent of Gassan. Already the remains of snowdrifts were visible in the valleys. Because we traveled by truck on the recently developed road, they did not visit the sites of the third, fourth, and fifth stations.

At 5:30 A.M. the trucks reached the end of the road, the sixth station. At this point we left the trucks for the climb on foot, amidst deeper drifts of snow. About 6:15 the seventh station was reached after climbing up through brush and snow. The sixth station seemed to be past the tree line, and by the seventh station, there were no trees at all. The seventh station was marked simply by piles of brush, with no sign of a shrine. After a well-deserved rest, we proceeded.

At about 6:45 we reached the eighth station. From the seventh to the eighth station a number of interesting sights appeared. The proxies passed some statues of Jizo and memorial stones in an area of the pilgrimage path called Sainokawara. Sainokawara is an important feature of the "otherworld" tradition at various sacred mountains, representing the boundary that dead spirits must cross to reach paradise. Jizo is well known as the Buddhist savior of the dead. People of the surrounding region often dedicate memorial stones here for family ancestors, and pilgrims usually place rocks on these piles when they pass, as an act of devotion and to help spirits of the dead accumulate merit in the next life. From this point on, there were memorial stones and many rock piles built up by generations of passing pilgrims. But the proxies passed this area without stopping, until they reached the eighth station, also known as Midagahara, the plain of **Mida** (the Buddhist divinity Amida). The prayer of purification was repeated at a small wooden shrine here, which is protected from wind and snow by eight-foot stone walls. Then breakfast was eaten, topped off with tea from a skier's hut.

Even from the seventh station, the scenery was quite beautiful, with a view to the north of Mount Chokai, the highest mountain in northeastern Honshu. Other mountains, such as the famous skiing mountain Zao to the east, came into view near the summit of Gassan. From below the eighth station skiers were seen. Gassan is one of the mountains famous for late spring skiing, but of course skiing is a modern innovation that disregards the religious ceremony called mountain opening. Traditionally, priests stayed on the mountain only during the summer pilgrimage season (because Gassan is uninhabitable in winter); these priests ceremonially "opened" the mountain to pilgrims when they entered the mountain in spring, and it was understood that people should not climb the mountain before the official opening. To a Westerner like myself, the vision of parka-clad skiers and white-clad proxies together presented an interesting contrast. There appears to be a contrast of West and East, new and old, secular and religious, but as the two groups drank tea together, it was difficult to draw any sharp line dividing them.

From this station the climbing became more difficult, and since the distance between the eighth and ninth stations is extraordinarily great, a rest was called in the snow at about 7:45. At 8:10 A.M. the ninth station was reached. Here there is a small shrine next to Bus-sho Pond, literally, "the pond where Buddhas live." The reference to Buddhas may mean *hotoke*, dead people who have become Buddhas, and surrounding the pond are various memorial stones. It is said that people bring cremation ashes here. Midway between the ninth station and the summit another rest was taken at 8:30, and at 9:00 the summit of Gassan was reached.

At the very summit is the tenth station, Gassan Shrine, entirely surrounded by an eight-foot wall of stone. Even though it was early May, heavy ice was on the nearby bushes. The proxies and others

Some of the proxies worshiping at the shrine on the summit of Gassan, the tenth sta-tion. This photograph, taken from atop the eight-foot wall of stone, shows the corner of the shrine roof at the right.

gathered inside the stone enclosure before the small shrine. As the prayer of purification was repeated, several bottles of sake brought along were offered and candles were lit. Later I was told that one feature of this ceremony was to divine the next year's crop or fortune by whether or not the candles stayed lit or went out during the recitation of the prayer.

If there is bad weather during the celebration of spring mountain, the proxies go directly from the tenth station of Gassan to Dewa Shrine on Mount Haguro. However, in 1964 the weather was remarkably clear, so the group of sixteen proxies, several voluntary participants, and I made a side trip from Gassan Shrine to Yudono Shrine. Because there was little time, all set out at once. A very rapid descent was made down the steep slopes of snow, part of the time by turning up one's toes and "skiing" on one's heels. One steep cliff was traversed by means of a steel ladder. As others have remarked, this object of worship, a natural formation of outcropping rock, resembles the torso of a nude woman. It is stained red by the hot springs that gush forth even in winter. Again the participants gathered before the stone to recite the simple prayer of purification. While resting and eating, various people drank the hot spring water, supposedly a healing cure, even though it had the characteristic "rotten egg" odor of hydrogen sulfide. Others dipped the tip of their white surplice in the water, or soaked their feet by standing in the running hot water. (Since they were wearing straw sandals, the water passed right through and warmed their feet.) Several bottles were filled with the spring water to take home. Some of the men paid respects to their ancestors' spirits in a spot still hidden in the snow, next to the object of worship.

The ascent from Yudono Shrine back to the summit of Gassan was quite arduous and slow. The height of Gassan is 1,980 meters (about 6,494 feet), and 1,504 meters (about 4,933 feet) for Yudono. Since the shrine at Yudono is below the summit, this meant a rather sharp ascent of more than 1,500 feet up slippery snow. Finally the summit of Gassan was reached at about 1:30 P.M., and everyone was congratulated with sacred sake—sacred because it had been ceremoniously offered to the kami during the earlier prayer at Gassan Shrine. Before 2:00 P.M. the quick descent of Gassan started, following the same pilgrimage path as the ascent. Only one rest was taken, about three, at the eighth station, and there was no religious activity during the descent.

The trucks, boarded at the sixth station about four, went directly to Dewa Shrine on Mount Haguro, arriving at about five o'clock. Everyone went immediately to the Saikan ("Purification Hall") in their white clothes. Individually, the participants paid their respects at the altar inside the Saikan. Until 1962, it was the custom to spend this final night of the spring mountain in a rough shelter, but in 1962 it was moved to the much nicer quarters in the Saikan. As the name *gyonin*, "ascetic," indicates, these people are considered to be performing *gyo*, or "ascetism," in their tour around the mountain. This is why they must observe abstinence. Thus, moving from the rough shelter to the Saikan marks another weakening or relaxing of ascetism. The Saikan is a fine, spacious shrine structure with kitchen and sleeping facilities for the shrine's pilgrims and general visitors. After everyone had had a hot bath, a meal of celebration (with no meat or fish) was brought from homes in the village. Much sake was exchanged, a common village banquet the next night was discussed but not agreed on, and after more drinking and singing, everyone retired after 9:00 P.M. In previous times there was no bath,

Proxies reciting a prayer before the Tenyu Shrine on Mount Haguro on the final day of the spring mountain.

and they went to sleep with their clothes on in the rough shelter. In 1964, apparently to retain the idea of asceticism, they were limited to two blankets for two people, sleeping on the straw mats found in all Japanese homes.

May 5, the final day of the spring mountain, began early. By 4:00 A.M., everyone was rising, exchanging cups of sake, and finishing the remainder of the previous night's meal. About 5:30 A.M. the children of these men came from the village via the stone staircase to pick up the lunch boxes and excess baggage. Then at 6:30, everyone walked to the Tenyu Shrine near the rough shelter. The Tenyu Shrine is the small shrine that honors Tenyu, the most illustrious leader in the mountain's history. After repeating the prayer of purification, they moved on to Dewa Shrine to listen to the Shinto priests recite a shrine prayer. Then the priests blessed the participants by swinging a pole with paper tassels over the heads of the participants and poured sacred sake for everyone. The participants then revered the shrine of Prince Hachiko, legendary founder of this sacred mountain. Next, we descended the stone staircase to the village, where we were greeted and congratulated by villagers. The last group recital of the prayer of purification was at the shrine office just above the entrance to the stone staircase. Leaving the shrine office, the pairs of proxies (or ascetics) gradually went their own way, paying their respects at their own buraku's shrine; this is their tutelary shrine, the first shrine each visited as a baby. Then the two proxies from each buraku attended the reception party in their own buraku.

I was able to witness the reception party of the seventh buraku, which retains the older traditional form. The "reception party" in Japanese is *saka-mukae*. *Mukae* clearly means a "greeting" or "welcome," but many half-joking meanings have been attached to *saka*. A popular explanation is that it comes from the word *saka* for "slope," referring to the three steep sections in the stone staircase leading to Mount Haguro; another explanation is that saka is derived from the word *sake* (rice wine), since sake is a part of every welcome or party. But the original meaning surely goes back to *sakai*, or "boundary," that is, a welcome at the boundary of the village or buraku. Japanese scholars have analyzed this celebration of *saka-mukae*, or "boundary-welcome," which is widely observed to welcome back pilgrims from a visit to a distant shrine or temple. The most common practice is to go to the village boundary both to see

The two proxies and other men from the eighth buraku of Toge gathered for the boundary welcome on a small hill just outside the village. The "Gassan rock" mentioned in the text is just to the left of the man on the right side of the picture; they are facing Gassan, seen in the background.

off and to welcome back the proxies. The returning person was regarded either as sacred or as an actual kami; originally, the boundary-welcome was a religious rite in which villagers saw off and welcomed back the person who left the village and traveled to the world of the kami. In general the boundary-welcome represents a meeting between the sacred world, which the "ascetic" has just visited (or the sacred state he represents), and the profane world of the village.

Formerly, each of the eight buraku of Toge held the boundary-welcome on separate small hills or knolls outside the village. This hill or knoll was known as the *o-yama* ("mountain") of that buraku, or *saka-mukae-yama*, "boundary-welcome-mountain." At present only the seventh buraku retains the older custom; each other buraku gathers inside a house of that buraku. When the two proxies of the seventh buraku entered the village, not stopping at any house, they went to their "mountain" about ten-minutes' walk from the village. The "mountain" or knoll is not even fifty feet higher than the surrounding fields; it is covered with low brush and one taller tree at the top. About twenty men of the seventh buraku were waiting on top of the knoll, sitting on reed mats before a celebration meal. It was past 8:30 A.M. The shrine papers acquired from Dewa Shrine were placed beside a rock under the tree. This rock, called the "Gassan rock," had been brought from Gassan long ago to dedicate the seventh buraku's "mountain" to Gassan. After a short greeting, all faced the snowy form of Gassan on the horizon and chanted the familiar prayer. This was followed by the formal feast of the spring mountain during which the shrine papers (in place of mountain plants) were distributed to the buraku members. The "red rice" (rice cooked with red beans) that is served on special occasions (such as weddings) was served, along with other special foods. The proxies excused themselves after eating a little and returned to the village. That night there were additional feasts, concluding the celebration of spring mountain.

Interpreting the Spring Mountain Festival

This description of spring mountain provides a good example of a village festival, illustrating the unity and dynamics of Japanese religion in a concrete case. To interpret this festival, we should recognize first that it has its own dramatic unity, with several climaxes. The festival begins with the proxies climbing Mount Haguro on May 3, practicing abstinence and indicating their pure state as pilgrims with their white clothing and surplices around their necks. The start of the pilgrimage is sealed with the ritual drinking of sacred sake given the proxies by the Shinto priests at Dewa Shrine. The festival moves toward its first climax on May 4, when the proxies recite their prayer of purification at each successive station of Gassan. Reaching the summit of Gassan is a climax in several senses. Gassan is a sacred mountain, and climbing it is to come into contact with sacred space and the kami of Gassan. At the same time, it is the attainment of the tenth station, which in Buddhist terms is to leave lower forms of earthly existence and enter a heavenly state. Another climax of the festival, especially from the viewpoint of the villagers, is the boundary-welcome, when the sacredness of the proxies rubs off on the others, and the shrine papers brought from the mountain are distributed to members of each home. This is a climax because it brings the power and blessing of the festival to each home.

By interpreting the major aspects of this festival in the context of Japanese religion, we can see how the world view and dynamics of religion are expressed in a concrete example. The spring festival includes all of the aspects or "worlds" of Japanese religion: objects of worship (kami, Buddhas, ancestors, and holy persons) as well as the religious ordering of social groups, space, time, and life.

The mountain kami of Gassan is the central object of worship for this festival, which symbolically brings the mountain kami to each village home in the form of shrine papers (which take the place of the traditional evergreens). Buddhas are also present on the mountain, especially in the statues of Jizo, savior of the dead, and in the area called the plain of Mida (Amida). Spirits of ancestors were venerated in several places, especially at the eighth station by the "pond where Buddhas live" and on Mount Yudono near the Yudono Shrine. In fact, some scholars think that the mountain kami and spirits of ancestors are similar if not identical. The proxies also honored a holy person when they paid respects at the Tenyu Shrine, honoring Tenyu, Mount Haguro's most illustrious leader. All these objects of worship played their roles in the drama of the spring mountain.

Religious ordering of social groups is expressed through families, buraku, and the village as a whole. Each of the eight buraku selected two male heads of families as proxies for the buraku; all proxies acted together to hold the festival for the village as a whole. Each home received a shrine paper as a symbol of the festival's blessing, and special rites were performed at each of the eight buraku shrines.

The religious ordering of space clearly specified certain locations around Toge as sacred space. Most important of all are the three sacred mountains, representing a kind of otherworld or heaven on earth. Also prominent are each of the ten stations leading to the summit of Gassan. On the village scene, in addition to the individual buraku shrines, there are the boundary-welcome-mountains, all of which are sacred space, too.

The religious ordering of time is demonstrated in the holding of the spring mountain on the eighty-eighth day of spring according to the lunar calendar. This is one of the major annual festivals for the village of Toge. In a larger sense, this festival is a collective action of the village to harmonize with the rhythm of the seasons and to open the agricultural year with a rite of spring.

The religious ordering of life is not prominent in this festival, which emphasizes collective action rather than cradle-to-grave rituals or individual practices. But because only male heads of families can participate as proxies, the festival is both a recognition of adult male status and a promise of future recognition to the young boys of the village. Even in small matters, such as the abstinence a man must observe while a proxy, it is obvious that this festival partially determines how these participants behave—what they can do and what they cannot do.

For the sake of analysis, this festival has been broken down into aspects or "worlds." But it is well to remember that the villagers of Toge do not experience religion through such analytical categories. Rather, they view the spring mountain as a precious tradition handed down to them, something they want to preserve and pass on to future generations. The participants told me this while they were celebrating on the night of May 4 in the Saikan, when they were drinking sake, dancing, singing, and having a good time. As the evening wore on they became more free in their conversation. Some of them had been in the Japanese military during World War II, and they assured me that Japan and the United States should not fight again but should be friends. They also told me that they were glad I had come on the festival with them, to see and record their tradition. They treasured this tradition and asked me to tell Americans not to send Christian missionaries—the people of Toge would preserve and respect their traditions, and Americans could follow their own traditions.

A proxy from the seventh buraku told me that having their young sons climb the stone staircase the next morning to take home some of the proxies' extra belongings was really not necessary, for these few belongings could be carried by the proxies themselves. Actually, he said, it was part of their sons' "education," to help them become a part of the spring mountain so that when they were heads of families they too would take their turns as proxies and keep alive the tradition. These comments helped me appreciate the importance of this festival for the people of Toge.

The spring mountain festival has changed through the years and will continue to change as long as it is practiced. The important thing to remember is that these villagers treasure the festival and intend to hand down this tradition to their children. The same kinds of feelings and intentions are associated with village festivals in other areas of Japan, as well as with festivals held in cities.

The Life History of Mr. Negishi

The two examples of religious dynamics have been chosen partly because they represent quite different expressions of Japanese religious life. Spring mountain, the first example, is a traditional festival as it has been handed down by a village in an agricultural setting. The second example, the life history of a Tokyo member of a New Religion, presents a sharp contrast with the spring mountain: it is part of the recent wave of new religious movements, takes place within the largest metropolitan area in Japan, and is a personal statement (as contrasted with the collective action in spring mountain). But in spite of these differences between the two examples, there are also many similarities, as we will see.

During the past century and a half Japanese society has undergone considerable changes, especially a shift from a rural and agricultural way of life to an urban and industrial way of life. One aspect of this change has been a weakening of the village community and the decline of festivals like spring mountain. Another aspect of this change has been the emergence of many New Religions, such as Tenrikyo and Soka Gakkai mentioned in Chapter I. As traditional village structure weakened and collective participation in activities such as village festivals declined, New Religions became increasingly important. Many people moved from rural areas to cities, in the process disrupting the tie between the family home and a local tutelary kami. This is just one instance of the general weakening of participation in traditional forms of religion. People who were separated from these traditional forms of religion often became involved in New Religions. Although New Religions incorporate many elements of traditional belief and practice, they are newly founded religious groups that individuals or families can join by their own choice. Previously, most religious life was not so much a matter of individual choice as a matter of residence and hereditary custom: a family participated in the local tutelary shrine where the family lived, and the family participated in the Buddhist parish temple designated by family custom. What is most "new" about New Religions is that a person or family makes a decision to join a particular New Religion, not on the basis of residence or family custom, but on the basis of personal preference for that particular New Religion.

Although each New Religion has its own distinctive history and set of practices, some features are common to most of them. They are founded by powerful personalities who are able to attract others to the message each has discovered. This message usually consists of elements from Japanese religion that are reformulated and systematized through a decisive experience of the founder, such as a revelation. As the founder gathers together people who are attracted to this message (and personally devoted to the founder), an institutional arrangement of headquarters and branch groups emerges. People become members of these New Religions, replacing (or adding to) traditional practices with the rituals and festivals that form a daily and annual pattern for each New Religion.

This example focuses on **Gedatsu-kai**, the New Religion joined by Mr. Negishi, whose life history provides us with an "inside" view of how a person joins and participates in a New Religion. Gedatsu-kai was officially founded in 1929 by Eizo Okano. Previous to his founding of Gedatsu-kai, Okano had a traditional upbringing and was familiar with the customs of Japanese religion, but he was more concerned with becoming a successful businessman than with religious life. Then, when he was forty-three, he was very ill and eventually lost consciousness. In a dreamlike state, which he experienced as death and passage to the otherworld, he met the spirit of his dead father, and the power of kami and Buddhas was revealed to him. He considered his recovery from this illness a miracle of new life made possible by the kami and Buddhas. This experience forced him to rethink his life and stimulated him to practice religion more seriously. The name Gedatsu-kai comes from *gedatsu*, meaning "liberation," similar to the term *nirvana* (usually translated "enlightenment"), and *kai*, meaning "society" and Okano felt he had experienced liberation or enlightenment (*gedatsu*), so he called his movement the "liberation society."

Gradually Okano left the business world and entered the world of religion full-time, telling others about the message he had discovered. He felt that too often people disregard religion or mechanically go through the motions of religious practice but do not reflect deeply on the meaning of life and the nature of religion. He realized that people owe everything to kami, Buddhas, and ancestors and should pray sincerely to them. Okano taught that many of people's problems in daily life stem from neglect of such worship, especially disregard of ancestors.

He was skillful in counseling people with personal and spiritual problems and quickly gained a following. Eventually the following developed into an institutionalized religion with central headquarters and local branches. But Gedatsu-kai teaches that membership in Gedatsu-kai should not interfere with traditional religious practices, in fact, Gedatsu-kai members should intensify participation in the local tutelary shrine and parish Buddhist temple. Gedatsu-kai has its own distinctive rites, such as a daily rite for honoring family ancestors in individual homes; it also features regular worship services and occasional meditation sessions in local and regional meetings. Okano died in 1948, but the movement he founded continued to grow, expanding to more than three hundred local branches and several hundred thousand members in Japan.

Mr. Negishi is a member of Gedatsu-kai who told me about his experiences. We first met in 1969 when I began studying Gedatsu-kai, and we met again during 1979–80, when I spent a half year studying Gedatsu-kai more thoroughly.[9] Part of this research was the recording of "life histories" of individual members, focusing on their religious experience. A life history is a personal story of how one remembers and interprets the course of one's own life. It was easy for Gedatsu-kai members to tell me their life histories, because a common practice in their meetings is for individuals to tell the other members present the story of their problems and how they resolved them. Mr. Negishi's life history is one of many I collected during 1979–80. This kind of personal narration is about as close as non-Japanese can come to seeing how a Japanese person experiences and lives out religious life today.

Mr. Negishi (a fictitious name used to protect his identity) was born in Tokyo, is a college graduate who lives in Tokyo, is financially independent, and donates much of his time to Gedatsu-kai. He has long been a member of this movement and now is an important member of the executive board of Gedatsu-kai. At the time of the interview, January 26, 1980, he was fifty-one years old. Mr. Negishi told his story in Japanese, which is translated into English here. The general import of his story is that religion is power, and the rationale for him to join Gedatsu-kai and participate in it is that Gedatsu-kai affords him the power to live. But it is best to let Mr. Negishi tell his own story. To retain the vividness of this personal document, it is quoted here in the first person singular—the "I" is Mr. Negishi talking. (The few instances where the author interrupted with questions are indicated in brackets). Mr. Negishi speaks:

"I entered Gedatsu-kai after I was ten years of age—between ten and twenty. There was a neighbor, an older person who was in a bank. And our family had leased land to him. This was an area formerly called Musashino—now a part of Tokyo. I am a real native of Tokyo. From ancient times my ancestors were here. They had land and rented it out. So I had a connection of **karma** with this person.[10]

"I was still young at the time, and did not have much feeling for religion. But then there was our family situation at the time—our family was in poor health, and there was always someone sick. For example, my mother was sick for the longest period of time—she couldn't get out of bed for seven years. There were always two or three in the family sick, and it went on for ten years this way; I thought this was hard for my father.

"But religion—well, in popular language, this is called newly arisen religions. As opposed to established religion, in the last hundred years or so these 'newly arisen religions' had appeared as new forms of religion. And Gedatsu-kai seemed to be of a low level. This is how I felt about Gedatsu-kai. But I was told that the teaching was excellent in Gedatsu-kai. The bank person had encouraged my father to go to Gedatsu-kai, but my father didn't want to go, so I went instead.

"I didn't like religion. Yet, at the same time, I was wondering about religion. In this world . . . in this world . . . is religion necessary? I thought, like most people, that what is most needed in the world are such things as politics, economics, and authority or power. In this light, in this world, religion is not really good, necessary.

"But there were problems in this way of thinking. For example, if a law changes, then good and bad change overnight—what was good according to the law yesterday is bad according to the law today. This was just after Japan's defeat at the end of World War II, and we had no power.

"At present young people, internationally—in Russia, everywhere, in all major countries—ask: What power does religion have? What purpose does religion serve? I thought this way, too—like all young people—at this time. Those who have power change their approval of religion, and the like, overnight.

"Of course, people said that if you believed, it would be bless-ing—you would get well, and so on.

"There are three main types of suffering: first, economic; second, feelings, that is, the family and human relations; and third, the body, that is, sickness. To resolve these problems of suffering, you should study religion, they said, but . . . . Throughout the world, there is religion. People always fight, even over religion, I thought. Most wars are religion-based. War is an argument among different peoples.

"The bank person was a fine person, so my father told me to go study Gedatsu-kai. I was against this. I had a sibling, an older sister, and because my mother was always sick, my older sister was like a mother. So my father told my older sister, too, to go study; and because my older sister was more gentle than me, she went, and I went, too. This was just after World War II.

"Even today the Japanese don't understand this. The Ise Shrine and Shrine Shinto were the cause of the war, so they say, but this is irrelevant. For example, the basis of religion, as we usually know it, is a teaching, ceremonies, propagation, rituals, and divinities—such as Buddhas. But this is irrelevant when we consider the practices of my family at the local tutelary kami. Where one lives—this is important.

"Emperor Ojin is the deity worshiped.[11] Also, there are lots of small shrines, lots of spirits, but Emperor Ojin is the chief kami. My ancestors were venerating these spirits, opened up this faith. So I followed the flesh of my parents. I had this tradition. My religion I did not think of as an acquired 'faith.' My ancestors were born of this earth, they were part of the realm of nature. We must be in harmony with the realm of nature. In other words, the realm of na-ture is equal to a kami. It is nature that allows us to live. We must live in harmony with nature. This is the basic thinking of Japan.

"Gedatsu's teaching is the same. It has the same view of nature. It emphasizes the local tutelary kami. And it stresses Buddhism. But Buddhism means our ancestors, as well as such divinities as the Buddha—this is how Japanese Buddhism is characteristically differ-ent from the Buddhism of other countries. So naturally Gedatsu-kai emphasizes the local Buddhist parish temple. So I was sympathetic to Gedatsu-kai.

"I wondered about life, what a human being is. I was twenty-two years of age when my father died. While my father was alive—and then relatives, and even neighbors—they said about business dealings and work, you must not do bad things, you must be honest. And they helped me affirm this. My father died, but before he died he had taught me, and I remembered his words and sentences, about not lying, keeping promises, and so forth. But as I said before, I had been wondering about human beings, and how they can live. I thought that humans do not have power. But one must have power. To protect oneself, and one's family, one must have power. But what is one's own power? It does not just come from one's own circumstances. How do you get power? How can one maintain power?

"In the teaching of the founder of Gedatsu-kai, and in Buddhism, there is the law of cause and effect. It is destiny. I studied genetics in the university. This is the scientific way of explaining it. The parents and children are the same—this is a genetic principle. 'The actions of the parents are passed on to the children.' The actions of the parents become the 'result' of the children. Strong or weak, this is the karmic connection of the parent: the karma of cause and effect. This is the law of nature. This is the nature of the human race.

"I learned this at school and thought it had no relation to religion—but then later I saw it in the founder's teaching! And was I surprised! The founder's disciples said that if I studied genetics, then I should understand the founder's teaching: 'If you studied genetics, then you ought to understand Gedatsu-kai.'

"There were many people who didn't go on the first and fifteenth of the month to the local Shinto shrine of the tutelary kami, but my family was a shrine parish representative. And my family went not only on the first and fifteenth of the month, but every day. From my youth, I went every day. My family is still parish representative. I myself don't participate that much as parish representative, but my mother, who is seventy-eight and healthy now, goes to the shrine as parish representative. I go to the local shrine of the tutelary kami for 'good morning' and 'good night.' My teachers in Gedatsu-kai said that if I did this, then I should understand Gedatsu-kai's teaching. In the morning, my 'good morning' greeting is, 'Again today your favor—blessing' in the evening, my 'good night' is, 'Thank you for another safe day.' I did this every day, as a custom, just as if I were greeting my parents.

Members of a local branch of Gedatsu-kai meeting in a home perform the purification of spirit that begins the goho shugyo ritual. Each member holds between joined palms a paper with a written Buddhist formula, as taught by the founder of Gedatsu-kai.

"Then there is another very important aspect of Gedatsu-kai's teaching, completely different, that I studied. As you know and as I have pointed out before, Japanese Buddhism is Mahayana Buddhism.[12] And this is fine, but in terms of human life, is the soul eternal? Worship is OK, but are there really kami? This is a doubtful matter. They say that even if the body is gone, people become kami. Is there a soul? Occasionally I practice the mediation ritual of **goho shugyo**.[13] I thought the teaching was wonderful but didn't believe in the practice of goho shugyo.

"I was told to practice goho shugyo. The branch leader of Gedatsu-kai and others urged goho shugyo. Many times I was told this. At first when I practiced goho shugyo, there was no spiritual communication. Then suddenly I had a spiritual experience; this was after many practices of goho shugyo.

"In the plain around Tokyo there was one family named Toshima that had pioneered the area. This was one major family, like the Chiba, Itabashi, Akasaka families, who opened up the plain around Tokyo, and whose family names became place-names. There was also a man named Ota who built the Edo castle. There was a long battle between the Toshima and Ota families, and the Toshima family lost out. This was at the end of the Heian period [794–1185]. The fallen Toshima had a residence at Shakujii—located in Nerima ward of present-day Tokyo. I saw all this during the ritual of goho shugyo. It lasted for fifteen minutes. I saw the entire struggle, the landscape, and everything. This greatly surprised me.

"There is only a little literature on this historical affair; Tokyo

University has this literature. And there is some information in the
Nerima local history. I saw all of this because I am a native of the
area. It is only eight—or six—kilometers to this place Shakujii from
my house, and to the site of the Toshima mansion, it is only one
kilometer. My relatives all live in this area.

"So the upshot is that the practice of goho shugyo and the study
of literature are all the same—in my heart I didn't know this before.
I didn't know it, I practiced the sacred goho shugyo and learned
about history. Later I read literature and was surprised to find this
experience confirmed. I heard their voices, the playing of the flute. I
still remember it clearly today. So several hundred years pass, but
souls still live—in our heart. They still express this through us. We
are conscious of them. The soul is immortal.

"And so I became quite interested in this. And the meaning may
be a little different here, but I saw this in other families: 'Ah, because the father did such and such, the child becomes so and so.'
And because I am a native of the area, and mine is an old family, I
know five or six generations of neighboring people—I can even recite the names of the heads of neighboring families going back that
many generations. And I see the influence of older generations in the
present. The suffering older generation affects the present generation, too. This is genetics.

"And when we rejoice, the ancestors do, too; this is because the
ancestors are the same as kami. The soul is immortal. This is the
essence of how things should be. Do good today, and it becomes
tomorrow's blessing. Today's evil, tomorrow's sorrow. And it is not
just oneself, but one's child, and grandchild. It is the divine provi-
dence of nature. A mistake goes back to the kami. A white flower
should be the same for three generations, and so on—it all goes
back to the same source. And a human, even if he makes mistakes—it all returns to the kami!

"The realm of nature is the 'way' the kami have created.[14] And
we must live according to the principles of nature. For example,
there are the sacred teachings of the founder—how man can live—
there is destiny. But what is humanity? It is as a human being that
the kami have created man. And it is according to this destiny that
one matures and lives. And because we have this human quality, we
must live as humans. And human nature—human quality, this
quality—knowing this is a level of maturing, a level of learning,

therefore we must practice this 'way.' We must study, practice, this 'way.' We must study, practice, learn. Thus we make happiness for others. The kami make everything: objects, persons, principles. We should give thanks for food—help create happiness for others. We have karmic connection with all things. We give thanks to the kami for this day, for everything.

"In our own hearts we grow and can understand this. Questions of what denomination we belong to, what sect—these are not important.

"For example, even if I take but one grain of rice and eat it, then it will never enter anyone else's mouth—this life was given just for my existence. For this we are very grateful! We must see that every day we live is given by the kami. To take good care of parents is the same thing. This is gratitude. And by this we know that it is due to the kami's heart that man lives.

"In our own hearts, we grow, and can understand this. Questions of what denomination, what sect—it is not just what is 'correct' according to the kami, or what the Buddha does not allow—rather, everything depends on the people, and the locale, and living in terms of this. Because this is what enables us to live. For example, take a teacup. We can use it to drink tea, or we can throw it at an enemy. So it is not the orthodox teaching, but the social, local relevance. We are enabled to live.

"So our power comes from the generations of ancestors. This is genetics. So for the descendants this is extremely important for their fortune. It is what the ancestors have done for us."

Interpreting the Life History of Mr. Negishi

As we attempt to interpret this human document, it is interesting to note that, like the spring mountain festival, this life history has its own dramatic unity. In this case, the drama centers around Mr. Negishi's personal quest for meaning. In childhood Mr. Negishi participated naturally in traditional religious practices, visiting the local tutelary shrine for a "good morning" and "good night" just as if he were greeting his parents. But in his teenage years after World War II, there was a great deal of uncertainty, and he was unsure about the power that would help him live his life meaningfully. The answer came in the teaching and practices of Gedatsu-kai, which did not contradict traditional beliefs but expanded them into a total philosophy of life. Mr. Negishi considered the founder, Okano's, teaching about gratitude to nature, parents, and ancestors a significant reformulation of traditional notions. After he had accepted Gedatsu-kai teachings in principle, Mr. Negishi had a transforming spiritual experience in which he communicated directly with the other world. On the basis of reasoning out traditional practices, as well as on the basis of personal experience, Mr. Negishi found in Gedatsu-kai a way of life that provides him with power to live meaningfully.

This single life history cannot speak for all Japanese today, but it provides a valuable inside view of how one person became a member of a New Religion and continues to participate in it. If we interpret this life history in terms of the world view of Japanese religion, it is remarkable how closely it follows this pattern of objects of worship (kami, Buddhas, ancestors, and holy persons), as well as the religious ordering of society, space, time, and life.

Mr. Negishi honors the whole range of objects of worship. He greets the local tutelary kami morning and night, like his own parents. He senses a deep gratitude toward nature, which provides human beings with life. He regularly visits the local Buddhist parish temple, expressing his concern for both ancestors and Buddhas. Not mentioned explicitly, but practiced by Mr. Negishi, are Gedatsu-kai's morning and evening devotions in the home, which include veneration of the Gedatsu-kai triad of the kami of nature, a Buddhist divinity, and the founder, Okano. Ancestors are very important and should be ritually revered morning and night. As Mr. Negishi reminds us, we are totally indebted to our ancestors, and we are equally responsible to future generations. In Mr. Negishi's eyes, there is little difference between ancestors and kami, and nature is equivalent to kami. He also reveres the founder of Gedatsu-kai, Eizo Okano, a kind of holy person. All these objects of worship form the resources of power Mr. Negishi draws on to live his life more fully.

The ordering of social groups is somewhat different from what was seen in the village festival of spring mountain. In that case the village automatically functioned as a unit to perform the festival. In the case of Mr. Negishi, it took some time and persuasion before he finally agreed to participate in the new movement of Gedatsu-kai. But his participation was based on a conscious decision to join, a kind of decision not usually made in village festivals like spring mountain. In joining Gedatsu-kai, Mr. Negishi chose to share religious practice with others both in local branch meetings and in national meetings of Gedatsu-kai members. In this fashion, Gedatsu-kai (like New Religions generally) represents a significant reordering of social and religious units. However, membership in Gedatsu-kai does not cause Mr. Negishi to stop traditional practices; in fact, it reinforces active involvement in both the local tutelary shrine and the parish temple. Gedatsu-kai is not only a form of reordering social units but also a means of reinterpreting the significance of society. Like other members of Gedatsu-kai, Mr. Negishi could see, as the founder had taught, that both personal and social problems often are caused by disregard for proper social relations and proper rituals for ancestors.

The religious ordering of space according to Gedatsu-kai both reinforces traditional notions and develops some new features. Mr. Negishi does not mention this directly, but it is implied in his story. Gedatsu-kai presents a total philosophy that explains the significance of the local tutelary shrine and Buddhist parish temple. In this sense, traditional notions of sacred space, which had tended to decline, are given new support. In a similar sense, the home is reinforced as a sacred site, not merely because of the presence of kamidana and butsudan, but also because Gedatsu-kai practices daily veneration of ancestors in the home with a distinctive ritual. One of the new aspects of sacred space in Gedatsu-kai is that the native village of the founder has become a sacred headquarters and holy site of pilgrimage. In this way, the traditional village religion of the founder has become a "national" village tradition for all members of Gedatsu-kai.

The religious ordering of time within Gedatsu-kai, as with its other key features, combines old and new. The traditional daily pattern of ritual is reinforced with specific Gedatsu-kai rituals in the home, especially the honoring of family ancestors. A new pattern that Gedatsu-kai has laid down is regular monthly meetings on both the local branch level and the regional level. This is more like an institutional "church." Gedatsu-kai has its own annual religious calendar, combining traditional festivals such as the New Year, spring festival, and fall festival with its own distinctive celebrations (for example, the anniversaries of the birth and death of the founder).

The religious ordering of life in Gedatsu-kai has some aspects of "cradle-to-grave" not mentioned by Mr. Negishi—such as special youth groups. But the major organization of life in Gedatsu-kai is a reformulation of traditional notions into a complete philosophy of life. Gedatsu-kai incorporates traditional practices at both the tutelary shrine and the parish temple with a renewed sincerity. Also, Gedatsu-kai helps people understand the karmic connection they have with all others, and how to behave properly toward other people. A person's life is not merely a biological fact but is granted by kami and nourished by ancestors.

Mr. Negishi's story has its own dramatic unity. The story has been broken down into various components to help us better understand various aspects of the world view of Japanese religion. But Mr. Negishi experiences the dynamics of Gedatsu-kai as it helps him resolve the problem of meaning, providing him with a total philosophy of life. This same theme is found in all the life histories of Gedatsu-kai members I collected during 1979–80.[15] Such a life history is a good illustration of the dynamics of religious experience in contemporary Japan, especially within the highly successful New Religions.

CHAPTER VI

Conclusion: The Contemporary Religious Situation

T he Japanese religious tradition is so rich and varied that many aspects cannot be mentioned in such a brief treatment as this book. Previous chapters have surveyed some key aspects of this tradition: the outlines of Japanese culture and Japanese religion, the historical development of Japanese religion, the world of worship, Japanese religion's world view, and two examples of religious dynamics. There is much more to Japanese religion that is not included in these few chapters, but before we leave the subject, it is well to ask what the religious situation is in Japan today.

The Sacred Way in Modern Japan

The general picture of Japanese religion is that it features many separate traditions, such as Shinto and Buddhism, within one sacred way. In the celebration of a village festival or in the personal story of a member of a New Religion, there is not just a single tradition or a combination of traditions but a total way of life that draws on all these resources. The spring mountain festival has its own dramatic unity that is re-created every time it is celebrated. And the personal drama of Japanese religion is re-enacted every time a person enters a New Religion—simultaneously resolving an individual quest for religious meaning and reformulating traditional practices. This is part of the total religious heritage in Japan—in other words, the "sacred way of Japanese religion."

This is the general picture of Japanese religion, but what are the problems and possibilities facing religious life in Japan today? Is the "sacred way" a remnant of the past, likely to fade away in the near future? What are the pressures that modern Japan places on religious commitment, and what changes are likely to take place within this sacred way? There is no one, either in Japan or outside Japan, who can answer such questions completely, because this is a matter of speculation about the future rather than a description of present or past. However, we may prepare for the future by reflecting on the possibilities that are suggested in the past and present of Japanese religion. There seem to be three major possibilites for the unfolding of religion in Japan from the present moment. One possibility is the continued practice of traditional religion. A second possibility is the further success of recent movements such as the New Religions, which develop somewhat different patterns than traditional religion. A third possibility that should be mentioned is choosing not to be religious—practicing no religion at all.

The first possibility, continued practice of traditional religion, is the extension of practices that have been very important during the past few centuries, such as maintaining a kamidana or butsudan within the home and venerating kami and ancestors. This "traditional" possibility includes religious activities carried on within a family, a village, or a section of a city as part of the collective social and religious life, much as was seen in the spring mountain festival. Obviously there are factors in modern Japan that make it difficult to continue these traditional practices as they were carried out in the past.

A key component of the sacred way throughout Japanese history has been the sacredness of kami. One modern factor that interrupts the traditional worship of kami is the changing life-style, especially the shift from a rural-agricultural way of life to an urban-industrial one. Many of the beliefs and practices associated with kami were directly related to agricultural activities. The spring mountain festival was considered the beginning of the rice growing season, ushering the mountain kami into the rice fields. However, many young people have left agriculture and taken jobs in the cities. For these young people, who may work a forty-hour (or more) week in a factory, it is difficult to recapture the traditional sense of the seasonal rhythm of spring and fall, with their appropriate spring and fall festivals. Factory workers are more likely to be concerned with leisure time on weekends and vacations than with the periodic "break" provided by festivals. It is not surprising that fewer Japanese homes today have kamidana, and that those that do have kamidana observe fewer ceremonies at the kamidana. It is obvious that for many contemporary Japanese people, the sense of the sacredness of kami is not the same as it was for farmers living in a traditional village some time ago.

This is one illustration of how "traditional religion" is changing. The earlier notion of kami and practices associated with it may be continued, but not exactly as they were in the past. Some changes may be minor, as some of the changes in the spring mountain: village representatives still venerate the mountain kami of Gassan, but they make the trip by truck, rather than on foot. Other changes, such as the dying out of some customs and festivals, are more significant. Changes may occur in how kami are perceived, and, in fact, have taken place through the centuries. As cities grew, some kami formerly associated with fertility and agricultural festivals came to be associated with good luck in business. In a case like this, the veneration of a particular kami is continued, but its significance is reinterpreted.

Undoubtedly some practices will survive and flourish: although many homes do not have kamidana, it is still a widespread custom to have butsudan. Some family and village ceremonies will continue, in spite of the difficulties. Some practices die, some flourish, and others continue in changed form. It is well to remember that "tradition" means something that is handed down from one generation to another. And whatever religion Japanese people hand down to their children is in this sense "traditional." One reason for the usual distinction between "traditional" and "modern" is that in times of rapid social change there is a greater degree of discontinuity and change in the culture that is handed down. This is the ambiguity of "traditional" religion in modern Japan: something will be handed down, but with a greater degree of change than occurred in the "handing down" several hundred years ago.

The second possibility is the further success of movements such as the New Religions, which represent considerable discontinuity from earlier religious tradition, such as village practices. The New Religions were founded outside the major religions and are alternatives to the almost automatic participation in tutelary shrine and parish temple. Joining a New Religion involves a conscious decision to enter a specific institution, like a "church." The same conditions that contributed to the disappearance or change in traditional religious practices have tended to help movements such as the New Religions continue and expand.

When people move from villages to cities and become rather separated from the agricultural way of life, they are more likely to join a New Religion. To put it the other way around, people who are caught up in village festivals and are participating as members of villages and families do not tend to join New Religions. It is especially people who see themselves more as individuals, or at least as individual families, who tend to make a conscious decision to join New Religions. This trend is likely to continue, because once the fabric of village life is torn, it is not a simple matter to reconstitute the earlier uniformity and cooperation of the village. One trend in modern Japan that is likely to continue is the movement of people both geographically (from area to area) and socially (from farm life to factory life and from one industry to another).

What are some of the implications of the success of the New Religions? It does not mean the end of Japanese religion but its transformation into new forms. While some kami may be neglected, other kami are reinterpreted and incorporated into the worship of a New Religion. A significant change brought about by these New Religions is the emphasis on the powerful personalities of founders, who are viewed as living kami. In the earlier centuries of Japanese religion there were holy persons, but the living kami of New Religions are more numerous and more prominent than the holy persons of medieval times.

The founder of Gedatsu-kai is revered by Mr. Negishi as the one who reformulated the many traditional practices into a more meaningful philosophy of life, setting up effective social groups (branches of Gedatsu-kai) and practical rituals for carrying out this philosophy. This newer style of social organization, with its emphasis on providing a total way of life in an explicit teaching, is one of the major contributions of the New Religions. However, as many scholars have pointed out, the New Religions are not completely "new";

in fact, they are mainly the reworking of old elements, such as veneration of ancestors, for example. This is another way of saying that as the New Religions come to be handed down to future generations (and not primarily joined by individuals through conscious decision), they in turn become "traditions," and all the New Religions as a whole may eventually become "traditional religion" as they become a major channel for transmitting earlier beliefs like veneration of kami and ancestors.

The third possibility is that the Japanese may choose not to be religious, participating neither in the more traditional family and village religious activities nor in the newer forms found in New Religions. This is not only a possibility, but is for a large number of Japanese people today an actuality: they do not participate in religion, and are much more concerned with matters such as economic activities than spiritual advancement. Most Japanese share with other "modern" people—those who live in highly urbanized, industrialized, and commercial settings—a preoccupation with "getting ahead" in the world. In fact, the special term "economic animal" was coined by the Japanese to deplore the dominant drive for money and consumption in Japanese life today.

Religious leaders in Japan, especially within Buddhism and the New Religions, have joined the criticism of the "economic animal," either directly or indirectly. These leaders view with alarm the trend toward international dilemmas of pollution and warfare: they say that it is uncontrolled materialism that leads to pollution, and nationalistic greed and ambition for power that leads to war. In this light, modern people may enjoy a higher standard of living without finding true satisfaction and enjoyment of life. It is interesting that many surveys of Japanese people show a relatively low percentage of people who are active in religion but a relatively high percentage of people who say that religion is necessary for living a meaningful life. Therefore, a large number of Japanese people who are not involved in religion are either looking for religious solutions or are potential participants in religious activities. One of the ironies of modern life is that it does not free people from religion; in fact, it may help turn people to religion.

A common misperception of Japan is that as it becomes more "modern," it becomes more "westernized" and less "traditional." It is true that Japan has borrowed considerably from other countries—

and will borrow more in the future. But whatever Japan has borrowed from the West it has modified and adapted to Japanese culture and will keep on doing this in the future. The important thing
to remember is that two processes are occurring simultaneously: Japan is borrowing and adapting foreign technology and culture, and
Japan is continuing and modifying Japanese culture. Japan has refined Western technology (cameras and electronics, for example)
but has utilized aspects of Japanese culture to organize and manage
industry.

The present tradition of beliefs, practices, and customs consti-
tutes the distinctive Japanese heritage of religion—an ideal against
which human life can be measured. In Japan, as in other modern
countries, there will be a large number of people uncommitted to a
specific religion or not active in religious life. But the ideal remains
in the background and is handed down by people committed to and
active in religious life and is made available for others. Often people
who had no idea of becoming involved in religion face a crisis and
realize personal significance in the ideal that has been kept alive.
Just as Japanese religion is constantly changing, so is the life of every
individual Japanese: no one can predict when any individual will
turn to religion, but many Japanese admit the necessity of religion
and may become active when the time is ripe for them.

The modern scene in Japan is so complex that probably all three
possibilities for religion will continue to coexist in the future. In
some places the older forms of "traditional" religion will continue,
although changes inevitably will occur in the process of handing
down older forms. At the same time, new forms such as New Religions will probably expand, and their style of organizing religious
life may spread to other areas. It is likely that Shinto shrines and
Buddhist temples will come to depend more on the conscious decision of individuals and individual families to participate in their observances. And it is probable that the dominance of the urban-industrial way of life will help keep most people preoccupied with
economic matters rather than religious matters. However, this concern for the physical and material may wear thin and give way to
interest in the spiritual and religious.

Although no one can predict the exact religious career for specific
individuals, it can be safely assumed that Japanese religion will continue into the future. It will not be the same as it has been, but it

will be distinctively Japanese. Kami, Buddhas, ancestors, and holy persons will probably remain at the core of Japanese religion and continue to form a distinctive pattern or "sacred way" that has always been characteristic of the Japanese religious heritage.

Notes

1. Donald Keene, *Japanese Literature: An Introduction for Western Readers* (New York: Grove Press, 1955), p. 22.

2. This manner of interpreting religious material is demonstrated in the work of Mircea Eliade, such as his *The Sacred and the Profane: The Nature of Religion*, translated by Willard R. Trask (New York: Harcourt, Brace, 1959); and *From Primitives to Zen: A Thematic Sourcebook of the History of Religions* (New York: Harper & Row, 1967).

3. For more information on ancestors, see Robert J. Smith, *Ancestor Worship in Contemporary Japan* (Stanford: Stanford University Press, 1974), esp. pp. 84–85, for the example of saving memorial tablets from fire.

4. Hajime Nakamura, *Ways of Thinking of Eastern Peoples: India-China-Tibet-Japan* (Honolulu: East-West Center Press, 1964), p. 450.

5. George DeVos, quoted in David W. Plath, "Where the Family of God is the Family: The Role of the Dead in Japanese Households," *American Anthropologist*, 66, no. 2 (April 1964), pp. 300–317.

6. For a more complete account of annual events, see Hitoshi Miyake, "Folk Religion," in *Japanese Religion*, edited by Ichiro Hori (Tokyo: Kodansha International, 1972), pp. 126–32.

7. This festival is treated at greater length in my article "The Celebration of Haru-Yama (Spring Mountain): An Example of Folk Religious Practices in Contemporary Japan," *Asian Folklore Studies* 27, no. 1 (1968), pp. 1–18.

8. The Japanese word for mountain is *san*, and Gassan is literally "moon mountain": because Gassan includes *san* or "mountain" within its name as a proper noun, it will be referred to simply as Gassan.

9. This research, including other life histories, will be published in a book I am preparing.

10. This popular notion of "connection of karma" means a close social relationship that has its own destiny; Mr. Negishi uses this term several times during his story, especially to refer to the karma of family ancestors.

11. According to tradition, Emperor Ojin was the fifteenth emperor and reigned A.D. 270–310. Emperor Ojin is identified with Hachiman, a composite object of worship with both Shinto and Buddhist features.

135

12. Buddhism is usually divided into two major groups: the Theravada, or more strict monastic tradition, of south Asian countries (such as Sri Lanka), and the Mahayana, or more liberal tradition, now dominant in east Asian countries.

13. Goho shugyo is a ritual technique combining meditation and mediation with spirits of the other world, especially spirits of ancestors.

14. In this case, the "way" means a way of life, like a philosophy of life.

15. Another life history from this research already published is "Gedatsukai: One Life History and Its Significance for Interpreting Japanese Religion," *Japanese Journal of Religious Studies* 7, nos. 2–3 (June–September 1980), pp. 227–57.

Glossary

Amaterasu. See Sun Goddess.

Amida. One of the most popular Buddhist divinities, especially in Pure Land Buddhism; people who place their faith in Amida are enabled to be reborn in the paradise of Amida; abbreviated as Mida.

Ancestors. In Japanese practice, the spirits of the dead, especially in the male line of the family, who have been transformed by funeral and memorial rituals into benevolent sources of blessing for descendants.

Buddha. The historical person named Siddhartha Gautama, who lived in India during the sixth and fifth centuries B.C. and founded Buddhism. Also refers to Buddhist divinities.

Buddhism. A religion emphasizing enlightenment, founded in India by the historical Buddha (Siddhartha Gautama) about the sixth century B.C. and brought to Japan about a thousand years later, where it was adapted to Japanese culture.

Buraku. Subdivision of a village (as in the village of Toge); can also mean a small community or hamlet.

Butsudan. A Buddhist-style altar in the home, a lacquered or finished cabinet in the main room of the home in which Buddhist divinities and family ancestors are enshrined.

Christianity. Introduced to Japan by the Jesuit missionary Saint Francis Xavier in 1549 but banned in the next century; Protestant and Catholic missionaries reintroduced Christianity in the mid–nineteenth century.

Confucianism. A Chinese teaching emphasizing social harmony set forth by Confucius about the fifth century B.C.; it became an important guide for ethics and social relations in Japan.

Confucius. The Chinese philosopher (551–479 B.C.) who set forth a teaching emphasizing social harmony by a return to virtue; this teaching was the basis for the social and ethical systems known as Confucianism.

Enlightenment. A Buddhist goal, achieved by overcoming human suffering and "awakening" to a higher peace.

Folk religion. The beliefs and practices held and transmitted by the people apart from formal religions.

Gedatsu-kai. A New Religion founded in 1929 by Eizo Okano, emphasizing self-reflection and a return to traditional values, especially veneration of kami and ancestors; it has several hundred thousand members.

Goho shugyo. A ritual technique in the New Religion Gedatsu-kai combining meditation and mediation with spirits of the other world, especially spirits of ancestors.

Holy person. In Japanese religion, a person, such as a founder of a sect or New Religion, who in his or her lifetime and/or after death is an object of worship or mediator of power for many people.

Jizo. One of the most popular Buddhist divinities, known as the savior of the dead, especially the patron saint of dead children.

Kami. The Japanese term for spirits or divinities, which may include mythological figures, the power within natural objects, the emperor, or powerful religious figures; generally kami signifies anything sacred; the term *kami* can be singular or plural.

Kamidana. A Shinto-style altar in the home, a special high shelf in the main room of the home on which a miniature Shinto shrine and offerings are placed.

Kannon. One of the most popular Buddhist divinities, sometimes known as the goddess of mercy; there are a number of forms of Kannon that grant various requests to people.

Karma. A Buddhist term (in Sanskrit) whose formal meaning is the actions and the results of prior actions; in popular Japanese usage, it also means the destiny of social relationships, especially the destiny passed down by family ancestors.

Ko. Associations or clubs formed locally for the purpose of honoring a particular deity and making pilgrimages.

Kojiki. A Japanese mythological writing from the eighth century that records the ancient traditions of kami.

Lotus Sutra. One of the most popular Buddhist scriptures in east Asia, it teaches the possibility of enlightenment for all people through simple acts of devotion.

Mida. See Amida.

Nembutsu. Recitation of faith in Amida (*namu Amida Butsu*) as an act of devotion, especially in Pure Land Buddhism.

New Religions. The many new religious movements founded by powerful personalities during the last century and a half, such as Tenrikyo, Soka Gakkai, and Gedatsu-kai.

Nichiren. A form of Buddhism named after the man Nichiren, emphasizing absolute faith in the Lotus Sutra and Japanese nationalism.

Nihongi. A Japanese mythological writing from the eighth century that records the ancient traditions of kami.

Nirvana. The Buddhist term (in Sanskrit) for enlightenment.

Norito. Ancient Shinto prayers, still used in Shinto ceremonies.

Pure Land. A form of Buddhism emphasizing faith in Amida and rebirth in the paradise of Amida; developed in China and stressed by Japanese Buddhists such as Honen.

Shaman. A person (in Japan, usually a woman) who has undergone special training and is able to go into a trance and be a medium between this world and other worlds.

Shingon. A form of esoteric Buddhism brought from China to Japan by Kukai (Kobo Daishi).

Shinto. The Japanese religion that developed out of prehistoric practices, especially worship of kami, and became a national tradition.

Shogun. A military dictator; ruled Japan from late medieval times until 1867.

Shrine. A Shinto building where kami are enshrined and prayers and offerings are made to kami.

Soka Gakkai. A New Religion founded before World War II and refounded in 1950; emphasizing faith in the Lotus Sutra, it has attracted millions of followers since the 1950s and is the largest New Religion in Japan.

Sun Goddess. (Amaterasu). One of the most important Shinto kami, from whom the imperial line descended; now enshrined at the Ise Shrine.

Taoism. A Chinese teaching emphasizing return to nature or harmony with nature and generally associated with Chinese folk traditions of the almanac and cosmology; it became influential within Japanese culture.

Temple. A Buddhist building where Buddhist divinities are enshrined; scriptures are recited and rituals performed before the Buddhist divinities.

Tendai. A form of Buddhism emphasizing the Lotus Sutra and comprehensive philosophy brought from China to Japan by Saicho (Dengyo Daishi).

Tenrikyo. A New Religion founded by Mrs. Miki Nakayama in 1838, emphasizing purification of personal life in order to lead a joyous life; the first New Religion to develop a large membership and effective organization.

Tutelary kami. The guardian kami of local Shinto shrines, which protect the people living in the area around these shrines.

Yakushi. A popular Buddhist divinity, known as the healing Buddha.

Zen. A form of Buddhism emphasizing enlightenment through meditation; developed in China and stressed by Japanese Buddhists such as Eisai and Dogen.

■

Selected Reading List

(For a comprehensive annotated bibliography on Japanese religion, see below:
Earhart, Japanese Religion: Unity and Diversity, *pp. 213–54.)*

Anesaki, Masaharu. *History of Japanese Religion.* London: Kegan Paul, Trench, Trubner, 1930. Reprint. Rutland, Vt.: Charles E. Tuttle, 1963.

Drummond, Richard H. *A History of Christianity in Japan.* Grand Rapids, Mich.: Eerdmans, 1971.

Earhart, H. Byron. *Japanese Religion: Unity and Diversity.* 3rd ed. Belmont, Calif.: Wadsworth, 1982.

————. *Religion in the Japanese Experience: Sources and Interpretations.* Belmont, Calif.: Wadsworth, 1974.

Eliot, Sir Charles. *Japanese Buddhism.* London: Edward Arnold, 1935. Reprint. London: Routledge & Kegan Paul, 1959.

Holtom, Daniel C. *The National Faith of Japan: A Study in Modern Shinto.* New York: Dutton, 1938. Reprint. New York: Paragon Book Reprints, 1965.

Hori, Ichiro. *Folk Religion in Japan: Continuity and Change.* Edited by Joseph M. Kitagawa and Alan L. Miller. Chicago: University of Chicago Press, 1968.

————. *Japanese Religion.* Translated by Yoshiya Abe and David Reid. Tokyo: Kodansha International, 1972.

Keene, Donald. *Living Japan.* Garden City, N.Y.: Doubleday, 1959.

Kitagawa, Joseph M. *Religion in Japanese History.* New York: Columbia University Press, 1966.

McFarland, H. Neill. *The Rush Hour of the Gods: A Study of the New Religious Movements in Japan.* New York: Macmillan, 1967.

Matsunaga, Daigan, and Matsunaga, Alicia. *Foundations of Japanese Buddhism.* 2 vols. Los Angeles: Buddhist Books International, 1974.

Miyake, Hitoshi. "Folk Religion." In *Japanese Religion,* edited by Ichiro Hori and translated by Yoshiya Abe and David Reid. Tokyo: Kodansha International, 1972, p. 121–43.

Murakami, Shigeyoshi. *Japanese Religion in the Modern Century.* Translated

141

by H. Byron Earhart. Tokyo: University of Tokyo Press, 1980.

Ono, Sokyo. *Shinto: The Kami Way.* Tokyo: Bridgeway Press, 1962.

Saunders, B. Dale. "Koshin: An Example of Taoist Ideas in Japan." In *Proceedings of the IXth International Congress for the History of Religions.* Tokyo: Maruzen, 1960, pp. 423–32.

Tomikura, Mitsuo. "Confucianism." In *Japanese Religion*, edited by Ichiro Hori and translated by Yoshiya Abe and David Reid. Tokyo: Kodansha International, 1972, pp. 105–22.